ID0983670

Wanda Gág

Twayne's United States Authors Series

Children's Literature

Ruth K. MacDonald, Editor

Bay Path College

TUSAS 645

WANDA GÁG, 1940
Reproduced by permission of Robert Janssen and the Children's Literature Research Collections,
University of Minnesota Libraries.

Wanda Gág

Karen Nelson Hoyle

University of Minnesota

Twayne Publishers • New York
Maxwell Macmillan Canada • Toronto
Maxwell Macmillan International • New York Oxford Singapore Sydney

Wanda Gág
Karen Nelson Hoyle

Copyright 1994 by Twayne Publishers

All rights reserved. No part of this book may be reproduced or transmitted in any form or by any means, electronic or mechanical, including photocopying, recording, or by any information storage and retrieval system, without permission in writing from the Publisher.

Twayne Publishers
Macmillan Publishing Company
866 Third Avenue
New York, New York 10022

Maxwell Macmillan Canada, Inc.
1200 Eglinton Avenue East
Suite 200
Don Mills, Ontario M3C 3N1

Library of Congress Cataloging-in-Publication Data

Hoyle, Karen Nelson.
Wanda Gág / Karen Nelson Hoyle.
p. cm.—(Twayne's United States authors series. Children's literature ; TUSAS 645)
Includes bibliographical references and index.
ISBN 0-8057-3968-8
1. Gág, Wanda, 1893–1946. 2. Illustrators—United States—Biography. I. Title.
II. Series: Twayne's United States authors series ; TUSAS 645. III. Series: Twayne's
United States authors series. Children's literature.
NC975.5.G34H69 1994
741.6'42'092—dc20
[B]   94-7002
                                                                         CIP

The paper used in this publication meets the minimum requirements of American
National Standard for Information Sciences—Permanence of Paper for Printed Library
Materials, ANSI Z39.48-1984.

10 9 8 7 6 5 4 3 2 1

Printed in the United States of America.

NC
975.5
.G34
H69
1994

For
Robert, Rebecca, and Natalie Hoyle
and Ruth Rasmussen Nelson

Contents

Preface

Wanda Gág's name and her first children's book, *Millions of Cats,* are inseparable in children's literature. That combination is often the reading public's outer limit of knowledge about the woman from Minnesota. But Gág made other significant contributions to the genre. She created an alphabet story book, translated the Brothers Grimm fairy tales, and she excerpted her young adult diaries for an autobiography, *Growing Pains.*

Books and articles about Wanda Gág typically capture only a limited portion of her life. A comprehensive assessment will be possible only after the diaries covering the period from her arrival in New York City in 1917 to her death in 1946—only just made available in 1993—have been studied. The purpose of this book is to re-create the life of Wanda Gág as it pertains to her books for children. Other researchers will place her in the historic annals of American art.

I would like to acknowledge the assistance I received from individuals and institutions. Dr. Edward B. Stanford, former University Librarian, acquired Wanda Gág manuscripts for the University of Minnesota during the 1960s. Robert Janssen, the executor of the Wanda Gág Estate and husband of Wanda Gág's sister Dehli, not only provided first-hand insight but also donated significant Wanda Gág materials to the university. Gary Harm, who succeeded Janssen as executor in 1989, and his wife, Norma (Dolly), made their personal collection of Flavia Gag Papers available. Violet Dehn, Adolph Dehn's sister, loaned correspondence she owned from Gág to Adolph Dehn documenting their courtship and later friendship. Fellow Gág researcher Audur H. Winnan shared new information and pointed the way to resources and collections. She copied in block letters many diary entries from Gág's almost illegible script. Collector George Glotzbach sent his acquisition lists and photographs. I also express my appreciation to the Minnesota Historical Society, which holds substantive materials. Staff member Deborah Swanson searched for unfamiliar holdings, while her colleague Ann Regan shepherded the reprint of *Growing Pains.* Daniel Traister and staff at the Special Collections, Van Pelt Library, University of Pennsylvania, made special arrangements for my visit. Paul Klammer and Leona Kellett from New

Ulm, Minnesota, provided information about the Gag family, as did the current Brown County (Minnesota) Historical Society staff.

In 1982 the Children's Literature Association provided a fellowship toward travel to the Philadelphia Art Museum, to the Weyhe Gallery in New York City, and to Florida for interviews with Robert Janssen. The University of Minnesota granted a sabbatical for further research and writing. Deidre Johnson nurtured the children's literature collections admirably in my absence.

Special thanks go to Margaret Aerol, Deborah Biorn, Marilyn Hoegemeyer, Florence Johnson, John Lundquist, and Alan and Ruth Nelson for their advice on the manuscript. My husband, Robert John Hoyle, supported this project along with my other professional endeavors. Bob and our school-age children Rebecca and Natalie waited patiently for my late arrivals from the library, retiring from the word processor and more imaginative meals while this book was in progress.

Acknowledgments

I would like to thank the following for permission to reprint excerpts, which are cited further in the Notes and References:

Gág's diaries and letters to Carl Zigrosser in the Wanda Gág Collection by permission of Department of Special Collections, Van Pelt Library, University of Pennsylvania, and of Gary Harm, Executor of the Wanda Gág estate.
Flavia Gag Collection by permission of Gary Harm.
Letters by May Massee by permission of Terry F. Dammann and Penguin USA.
Wanda Gág and George Biddle Papers, by permission of Archives of American Art and of Gary Harm.
Reviews by permission of Junior Bookshelf.
Reviews and commentary by permission of The Horn Book, Inc., 14 Beacon St., Boston MA 02108.
Alma Olivia Schmidt Scott and Family Papers by permission of the Minnesota Historical Society and Gary Harm.
Wanda Gág Collection in the Children's Literature Research Collections, University of Minnesota Libraries by permission of University Libraries and of Gary Harm.
Letters by Rose Dobbs by permission of Rose Dobbs and of The Putnam & Grosset Group.
Letter by Wanda Gág to Lewis Gannett by permission of Houghton Library, Harvard University, and of Gary Harm.
Letter by Wanda Gág to the Children's Department by permission of Minneapolis Public Library and of Gary Harm.
Books by Wanda Gág, Coward-McCann promotional material, and letters by Thomas Coward and Alice Torrey by permission of The Putnam & Grosset Group.
Wanda Gág Inscription to Edgar Hermann by permission of Elizabeth Cowie.
Letter from James Giblin to author by permission.
Letter from Audur H. Winnan to author by permission.
Photographs by Robert Janssen by permission.
Letter by William C. D. Glaser by permission of University of Oregon Library.

The Putnam & Grosset Group also granted permission to reprint illustrations from these works:

Illustration by Wanda Gág reprinted by permission of Coward-McCann from *Millions of Cats,* copyright 1928 by Coward-McCann, Inc., copyright renewed 1956 by Robert Janssen.

Study by Wanda Gág reprinted by permission of the Children's Literature Research Collections, University of Minnesota Libraries (CLRC), and of Gary Harm for *The Funny Thing,* copyright 1929 by Coward-McCann, Inc.

Study by Wanda Gág reprinted by permission of the CLRC and of Gary Harm for *Snippy and Snappy,* copyright 1931 by Coward-McCann, Inc., copyright renewed.

Illustration by Wanda Gág reprinted by permission of Coward-McCann from *Snow White and the Seven Dwarfs,* copyright 1938 by Wanda Gág, copyright renewed 1966 by Robert Janssen.

Illustration by Wanda Gág reprinted by permission of Coward-McCann from *Tales from Grimm,* copyright 1936 by Wanda Gág, copyright renewed 1964 by Robert Janssen.

Chronology

1893 Wanda Hazel is born 11 March in New Ulm, Minnesota, to Anton Gag and Lissi (Biebl) Gag.

1908 Father Anton Gag dies 22 May, leaving wife with seven children ages one to fifteen.

1909 "Robby Bobby in Mother Gooseland" is published in *Junior Journal*, a supplement to *Minneapolis Journal*.

1910 Work is exhibited in traveling exhibit organized by Minneapolis School of Art director; receives bronze medal in contest sponsored by St. Paul Institute of Arts and Sciences.

1912 Graduates from New Ulm High School in June. Begins teaching school in Springfield, Minnesota in November.

1913 Completes teaching in late spring. Begins St. Paul Art School in October.

1914 Continues art school through May. Returns to New Ulm for summer and continues art school in fall. Transfers from St. Paul Art School to Minneapolis Art School in December.

1917 Mother Elisabeth (Biebl) Gag dies 31 January. Gág is responsible for herself and six younger siblings. Remains at Minneapolis Art School to complete studies until June. While in New Ulm during summer, illustrates *A Child's Book of Folklore*. Begins study at Art Students League of New York in October as scholarship student.

1918 Spends summer in New Ulm. Sells house and goods. Returns to New York City. Enrolls in class at Art Students League. Works as commercial artist.

1921 Joins Happiworks Company as artist.

1923 First one-person exhibit at East 96th Street Branch of New York Public Library opens in February. Abandons New York City and commercial work and moves to Connecticut to draw. Happiworks bankruptcy.

1924   Exhibits at same library branch in April.

1926   Participates in Weyhe Gallery Show in November.

1928   One-person exhibit opens at Weyhe Gallery in March. *Millions of Cats* published.

1929   *The Funny Thing* published.

1931   *Snippy and Snappy* published. Purchases farm in New Jersey; later names it "All Creation."

1932   *Wanda Gág's Story Book* published.

1933   *The ABC Bunny* published.

1935   *Gone Is Gone* published. Short story "The Cry Away Bird" published in *The Delineator.*

1936   *Tales from Grimm* published.

1938   *Snow White and the Seven Dwarfs* published.

1939   "I Like Fairy Tales" published in the *Horn Book.*

1940   *Growing Pains* published.

1941   *Nothing at All* published.

1943   *Three Gay Tales* published. Marries Earle Humphreys 27 August.

1945   Has exploratory surgery. Travels to Florida 24 December.

1946   Returns first to New York City and then to "All Creation," her home in New Jersey. Dies of cancer 27 June at Doctors Hospital in New York City.

1947   *More Tales from Grimm* and *The Book of Knowledge,* with her illustrations for "East of the Sun and West of the Moon," are published posthumously. *Horn Book* memorial issue.

Chapter One

What Father Began...
A Biographical Perspective
on Wanda Gág

Feature articles about Wanda Gág frequently refer to her as a Cinderella, someone swept from poverty to prominence by golden opportunities and circumstances. On the contrary, Wanda Gág planned continually and worked relentlessly to reach her goals. While her father never realized his dream of success as an artist, he challenged Wanda on his deathbed to fulfill hers. During a lifetime of little more than five decades, Wanda Gág achieved a notable reputation in both graphic arts and children's books. Her subject matter—hilly landscapes, dilapidated buildings, and foregrounds with animals, flowers, and domestic furniture—worked well in either genre.

Wanda Gág was a driving force in the lives of her family members and close friends. Her life was shaped by persistence, work, sacrifice, and success. She lost her father, Anton, when he was forty-eight years old and she only fifteen. When her mother, Elisabeth, died nine years later, with the youngest child only ten, Wanda Gág shepherded five younger sisters and a brother. Although she enjoyed the company of men, Wanda Gág postponed marriage until the age of fifty.

The lithe, dark-haired, brown-eyed Gág pursued her artistic talents in the Twin Cities of Minnesota and then on the East Coast. (It was soon after moving to New York City that she changed the spelling of the German family name, Gag, to Gág, in an effort to get easterners to pronounce it correctly. As she put it in a data sheet sent out along with letters to fans: "Pronounce it "Gaag"—to rhyme with jog, not bag please!" Wanda was the only one in her family to adopt this spelling.) After leaving the Midwest, she skimped while living in New York City and sent money to her sisters and brother who remained behind. Later she retained her professional contacts in New York City but retreated to her rural home in western New Jersey, named "All Creation," where she was occasionally joined by siblings and friends.

Gág's world encompassed children's stories and drawings as well as fine art. At a time when fellow Minnesotan Sinclair Lewis wrote scathing novels about hypocritical American mores, Gág fought for her status as a woman artist, producing her most remarkable drawings and prints during the 1920s. *Millions of Cats,* a children's book published in 1928, remains an American touchstone today. Gág worked relentlessly right up to her untimely death from cancer at the age of fifty-three.

New Ulm

Wanda Gág was born 11 March 1893, in New Ulm, eighty miles southwest of the Twin Cities of Minneapolis and St. Paul and considered the most German of Minnesota towns. At the turn of the century, 20 percent of its 5,403 citizens claimed Germany as their birthplace.[1] But diversity was evident in the religious tolerance that prevailed among Catholics, Protestants, and Freethinkers. Wanda's father, Anton Gag, had emigrated from Neustadtl Bei Heid in Bohemia and later affiliated with the Freethinkers, who met at Turner Hall. Meetings at the hall served as the stimulus for socialist and intellectual discussion, as well as a place for athletic training.

Anton Gag's hope was to make a living as a painter. His favorite subject was the Dakota (Sioux) Indian; a painting of the Indian Massacre of New Ulm survives in the Minnesota State Capitol. He empathized with the American Indians despite an assault on New Ulm during the uprising in August 1862, which resulted in the execution by hanging of thirty-eight Sioux on 26 December of that year. Occasionally Anton visited reservations to paint portraits, returning with deerskin clothing that he kept in his studio. The World's Columbian Exposition of 1893 in Chicago exhibited his panorama. To augment his limited income as an artist, he worked as a decorative painter and a photographer. He painted interiors of churches in Minnesota towns, including New Ulm, Mankato, and West Albany. A photographic studio, to which he was attached in various business arrangements, proved more profitable. He hired Elisabeth (Lissi) Biebl, a local woman born in Harrisburg, Pennsylvania, as a photographer's assistant. They married in June 1892. Their firstborn was Wanda Hazel, whom Anton called his "little black mouse" for her dark coloring. With the births of Stella Lona, Thusnelda ("Tussie" or "Nelda") Blondine, Asta Theapolis, Dehli ("Dale") Maryland, Howard Anthony Jerome (the only son), and finally Flavia ("Flops") Betti Salome in 1907, the children numbered seven.

In 1897 the family moved to a New Ulm house for which Anton Gag earlier had drawn plans; he had lacked sufficient funds to occupy it immediately. Neighbors frowned upon his "extravagances" of a skylight and wide windows. To add to the character of the house, Anton decorated the dining room ceiling with cherubs and walls with geometric motifs.

Like people in New Ulm, the Gag family spoke German at home, and Wanda first learned to speak English in public school. Unlike other families, the Gags did not attend church, and none of the children were baptized.

While Anton was a strict disciplinarian, both he and his wife, Lissi, gently encouraged art, literature, and music in the home. In the upstairs studio-library were art magazines and books, which the children could peruse. Anton played his zither weekly with a group at Turner Hall. Lissi differed from the neighborhood women. Artistic along with Anton, she designed and sewed for the older girls dresses with ruffles and lace. She posed them in these outfits for family photographs, suggesting an affluence that was far from reality. On the other hand, Lissi generally allowed the children to go barefoot and left their clothing unstarched. She even arranged the girls' hair in curls rather than braids.

Anton adored his daughter Wanda and taught her to draw before she was three years old. She therefore assumed that all children drew and wrote stories as a daily routine. Sometimes on Sundays he invited her to his top-floor studio, where he painted for his own pleasure. On occasion Wanda accompanied her father when he painted backdrops for amateur plays at Turner Hall.

While the town had Turner Hall and the public school, there was no public library during Gág's childhood and the school owned little extracurricular reading material. Gág later recalled, "We could only use our [school] library cards on Fridays, and there were so few books that before long we had read them all—after that there was nothing to do but read the same ones over again."[2] Her favorite childhood stories were "The Three Bears," "The Man Who Wanted to Do Housework," and the Grimm Brothers' *Kinder-und Hausmärchen,* or "Household Tales," read or told to her by members of her mother's family who lived on the outskirts of town. To visit those relatives, the children followed the railroad tracks through New Ulm's "Goosetown" (Ganseviertel) to the Biebl farm along the Minnesota River. "Nearly half my childhood memories center about activities in connection with the Grandma folks,"[3] Gág told Alma Schmidt, her childhood friend and future biographer.

Together with Olga Mayer or alone, Gág told stories and began writing them in earnest in sixth grade. Friendship with Schmidt, nicknamed

"Schmidty," began in high school and continued throughout adult life. They shared an appreciation of literature and music. The Schmidt family owned many books and magazines that the two girls read together and discussed. Gág admired the graphic artists Jessie Wilcox Smith and Harrison Fisher, whose work was prominent in her reading material. Both the Gags and the Schmidts had pianos, and the girls learned to play duets. When apart during summer vacations, the best friends corresponded by letter.

As the friendship flourished, the Gag family life moved toward crisis. In 1908, when Wanda Gág was fifteen, her father impulsively sold his decorating business. Not long after he died from tuberculosis. The youngest child, Flavia, was only a year old. On his deathbed, Anton challenged his eldest daughter: "Was der Papa nicht thun konnt', muss die Wanda halt fertig machen" (What Papa couldn't do, Wanda will have to finish).[4] At that time, Wanda Gág vowed that she too would become an artist. Anton Gag's modest insurance policy, along with $8 from welfare each month, was too meager to cover family expenses. Anton, however, left the Gag children another legacy—commitment to art. When townspeople suggested that Wanda Gág clerk in a store, she refused. She was determined that not only she but all her siblings would graduate from high school. Eventually all seven Gag children reached this goal, although Wanda delayed her own graduation to stay at home half-days. She managed the household and cared for the youngest children when her mother seemed unable to cope.

Lissi Gag, Wanda's mother, became an alcoholic after a well-meaning doctor prescribed beer to build up her strength.[5] Wanda Gág's adult diaries comment on her mother's frequent "illnesses." She reminisced about the regular arrival of the beer wagon and her mother's attempts to hide the beer and her drinking from the children. Physiology classes in school were a torture for the youngsters as they learned of the ravages of alcohol and saw the effects in their own mother.

At-home training in fine arts proved financially profitable for the Gag children. To augment the family income, the older girls made and sold artwork. Wanda herself taught art classes to children on Saturdays and created bookmarks cut from the deerskin clothing in the house, greeting cards, postcards, place cards, valentines, birthday books—all of which she sold to her teachers and to Eggen's Drug Store. One teacher, Miss Lee, paid her $1.50 for a birthday book (*Growing*, 49). Some people advised Wanda to charge more than 25 cents for a two-hour art lesson, but she considered a quarter fair payment. All the older Gag girls submitted drawings, stories, poems, and cartoons to magazines and to the *Minneapolis Journal,* which had a Saturday supplement called *Journal Junior.* As an adult, Wanda Gág recalled that the publication "encouraged the creative efforts of grammar and high school students by actually paying for accepted material, and I immediately deluged them with my work" (*Growing,* xx). During a period of eighteen months, Gág earned over $100, mostly from the pink-paged supplement (*Growing,* 69). To record the income, Gág used her father's ledger, which became her first diary.

Writing in consecutive diaries became a necessity, and even an obsession, which she continued most of her life. She bought student notebooks when younger and journal books in her adult life, and together they reveal her emerging and maturing personality. She used an ink pen or pencil, observing that pencil seemed easier for others to read. Gág liked to reread her diaries, but lost an occasional one either in transit or while on loan for someone else to read. She later selected entries from the first group of diaries as the basis of an autobiography, *Growing Pains,* published in 1940. Gág intended to write faithfully in her diaries, but there were long periods after her arrival in New York City when she summarized days or even months. She made entries even when she was terminally ill in 1945 and 1946. At seventeen she entered the following, which served as a theme for her life: "My Own Motto—Draw to Live and Live to Draw" (Diary 10, 28 October 1910).

From an early age, Gág received recognition for her achievements. From the age of fifteen to eighteen especially, her name appeared often in the *Minneapolis Journal. Journal Junior* editor Mae Harris Anson invited her to submit a series with text and illustrations for ten issues and offered Gág $50 for this project. "Robby Bobby in Mother Gooseland" appeared in the *Journal Junior* from 2 May to 4 July 1909.

Statewide recognition came to Gág when she was a seventeen-year-old junior in the New Ulm High School. Staff from two art schools in the Twin Cities of Minneapolis and St. Paul became acquainted with Gág. Professor Robert Koehler, director of the Minneapolis School of Art, organized a traveling art show that came to New Ulm in 1910. This was the first exhibit with Wanda's art, and it also included paintings by Anton Gag. The St. Paul Institute of Arts organized a contest for Minnesotans, administered in her area by *The Brown County Journal.* Gág received a bronze medal for two pencil drawings (*Growing,* 119). The *New Ulm Volksblatt,* a German language newspaper, covered the event and reprinted her drawings. Gág pasted the clippings in the first of two

scrapbooks, which she referred to as her "Blaa (Brag) Books." Gág continued the practice of collecting and assembling exhibition notices,
reviews, and special correspondence. The last clippings pasted at the end
of second scrapbook were dated 1938; afterward she merely placed clippings in folders.

Now Gág's horizons extended beyond New Ulm. She accompanied
her friend to St. Paul for several weeks on a visit to Schmidt's uncle and
aunt, Governor and Mrs. A. O. Eberhart. This gave Gág a taste for city
life. There the girls saw a production of *Macbeth* and rode a trolley car.
Gág had an interview with the St. Paul Institute of Arts and Sciences
business manager, Tyler McWhorter, who took her on a tour of the
school. He asked Gág if he might print her sketch of Mrs. Eberhart in
the *St. Paul Dispatch,* where he worked part-time as a cartoonist.

Gág wrote the class poem for her high school graduation in 1912, at
which President George E. Vincent of the University of Minnesota spoke
to the twenty-four graduates. Gág spent the summer studying to qualify
for teacher certification. At a "University Days" extension program, Gág
met Edgar Hermann, a student whom she would meet again when she
moved to the Twin Cities for art school. Gág became even more interested in the possibilities the Twin Cities offered. But because she needed an
income, she taught in a one-room rural school in Brown County near
Springfield in South Central Minnesota for the next school year, which
lasted from November 1912 through April 1913. After she paid living
expenses, she sent the balance of her salary to her family in New Ulm.
She was now twenty years old.

Twin Cities Art Schools

Gág's dream of attending art school eventually came to fruition, first in
St. Paul and then in Minneapolis, its twin city across the Mississippi River.
Assisted by monetary gifts from friends, a scholarship, and a part-time
job at Buckbee Meers as a commercial artist, Gág was able to enroll in
the St. Paul Institute of Arts and Sciences in fall 1913. Charles Weschke,
the brother of Gág's high school German teacher, paid her room and
board. He knew Gág from Springfield, where she had taught rural
school. (Weschke had became wealthy on patent medicine and as a drug
salesman.) At the year's end Gág won Second Honorable Mention in
illustration at the State Art Exhibit.

Gág's character developed at art school, as she concerned herself
increasingly with her appearance, her intellect, and social interactions.

Gág made many of her own clothes and wore a large hat and her father's Austrian cape. Without deliberately seeking friends, she soon found herself the center of attention at the Young Women's Christian Association (YWCA) where she lived. Gág made sketches of her new friends and gave the drawings as gifts. Her circle of friends included students at the university, and she occasionally read their books and discussed poetry with them. Men courted her. In a book loaned to her by one of them, she wrote, "I hope you will forgive me for having written in your books. I wrote them in pencil so you will have no trouble erasing them."[6] She then explained her urge to record her impressions, and enhanced the notes with sketches.

In December 1914, Gág transferred to the Minneapolis School of Art where she chose courses which would enable her to become an illustrator. Gág studied under Robert Koehler for three years; Gustav Goetsch was her favorite teacher. Canvases and oil paints seemed prohibitive in price until she received some financial assistance from *Minneapolis Journal* editor Herschel V. Jones, whom Gág called "the journal man." With other students, she drew and sold sketches of celebrities and opera goers to earn extra cash. She also drew illustrations for a University of Minnesota publication, the *Minnehaha*. During this time, she relied on her "drawing moods" and annoyed her teachers when she failed to complete her assignments.

Men were another source of diversion from her coursework. While she liked their company, she complained if they did not consider her their intellectual and artistic equal. To Schmidt, who was staying in Chicago, Gág wrote, "I have the most aggravating chance of becoming popular again. I do not wish that. It wastes energy and time, two things I can never have too much of" (Gág to Schmidt, 9 July 1915, MHS). She explained her concept of "Myself and Many Me's" to some friends. "Myself . . . stands for my better judgement, for my permanent self, and Me is my unstable self, the part that is continually changing" (*Growing*, 212). At twenty-two in 1915, she wrote to a young man, "I have more courage and self-assurance than many a man, and yet I am treated as a mere wisp of femininity. . . . I shall not rest until men are willing, and glad, to regard me as important as they (and with my hair hanging down my back in curls if I choose!)" (*Growing*, 421).

When her mother became seriously ill with pneumonia in January 1917, Gág returned to New Ulm and kept vigil at her bedside the night she died. Now head of the family, Gág felt responsible especially for the two youngest children, fifteen-year-old Howard and ten-year-old Flavia.

In the meantime, Gág and fellow classmate Adolf Dehn[7] were among twelve students to receive scholarships offered in national competition to attend the Art Students League of New York City. Dehn, from Waterville, Minnesota, and two years her junior, was more than a fellow student; he was her beau, whom she referred to as her "cavalier."

Returning to New Ulm in summer 1917, Gág illustrated Jean Sherwood Rankin's *A Child's Book of Folklore: Mechanics of Written English,* published by a Lutheran Synod to assist immigrants in learning the English language.[8] Gág's youngest sister Flavia and her cousin Delores posed as models for the book's eleven illustrations. Although townspeople talked about adopting the youngest children, the siblings wanted to stay together. Adolf Dehn helped to paint the family house to prepare it for sale. Because it did not sell, the final decision was that the four youngest children should stay in the home. Moving to Minneapolis, Stella worked in air-brushing and Thusnelda pursued business school.

New York City

In September 1917, Wanda Gág, Adolf Dehn, and Arnold Blanch left for New York City. She lived at the Studio Club, located near the Art Students League and run by the YWCA. Her goal was to become a magazine illustrator. At the Art Students League, Gág studied under Frank Vincent DuMond and Kenneth Hayes Miller. She took an evening etching class from Mahonri Young, a composition course from Robert Henri, and a class in advertising illustration.[9] In addition, she attended classes and lectures given by Ernest Haskell, John Sloan, and Charles Chapman, all of whom personally encouraged her.

In her free time, Gág explored New York, visiting museums and galleries and attending lectures, often with Adolf Dehn. Paintings by Delacroix and Cézanne at the Metropolitan Museum of Art appealed to her most. With her friends, she walked around the Palisades, Central Park, Chinatown, and Greenwich Village, and attended Christmas Mass at St. Patrick's Cathedral. They heard socialist lectures by Max Eastman and art lectures by George Luks and C. Lewis Hind. During this time, Gág met students Peggy Bacon and Yasuo Kuniyoshi and the sculptor William Zorach. Dehn socialized more than Gág, and she criticized him for it.

Finances were tight both for Wanda in New York City and for the youngsters in New Ulm. Although Twin Cities acquaintances sent money, her struggles with finances remained constant. Shortly after arriving in New York City as an art student, Gág made the rounds of publishers. She used the classified section of the telephone book to identify appropriate publishers, but to no avail. In December 1917 the family in New Ulm had only $30 to last through the winter. During that harsh winter, the Gág siblings conserved money and heat by living in only a few rooms of their New Ulm house. The pump froze, and sometimes they had no food. Gág wondered how to earn enough money to buy Christmas presents for the family.

Although she hated commercial art, she skipped some of her classes to work on design projects that would bring in cash. She visited the Charles Scribner's Sons publishing company, but despite encouragement, received no assignments. Buttrick's also expressed interest in her work, but the interviewer claimed that there was little demand for children's books. Registration at the Placement Bureau of the Art Alliance brought no results either. Having no success with publishers, Gág did manage to eke out a little income by posing in costume for an art class and for an individual artist and by painting lamp shades.

To further reduce expenses in New York, Gág and a girlfriend moved into another apartment, where they lived and slept in the kitchen. She sent the difference she saved in rent to her siblings in New Ulm. While Gág's "journal man" from Minneapolis was in New York City for business, he gave her $40 to buy clothes.

When the art school term ended in May 1918, Gág returned to Minnesota by train, renting a pillow instead of a sleeping compartment. She spent the summer in New Ulm. The judge of probate allowed the family to sell the house in New Ulm and move the siblings to Minneapolis. While awaiting occupancy of an apartment during the summer, the youngest children stayed in a tent on the Dehn farm in Waterville and then with Johan Egilsrud's family in Minneapolis. Gág traveled back to New York, enrolled as a scholarship student in only one course at the Art Students League (offered by DuMond), and sought commercial art work. She completed some advertisements for Best and Company and continued to paint lamp shades.

Gág Makes a Living, 1919–1925

At the end of World War I, Dehn, who had been drafted into the army in 1918, returned to New York. There he shared an apartment with Earle Marshall Humphreys, a friend from the army who, like Dehn, had been a conscientious objector, and artist friend John P. Flanagan. Gág's landlord criticized her for allowing men to stay in her apartment late at night. To save money, Lucille Lundquist, Violet Karland, and Gág often prepared meals with the three men. At this time Gág weighed less than 100 pounds; and although she was not a vegetarian, she considered meat too expensive. Her "social activities" included attending court hearings along with her male friends. Max Forester Eastman, editor of the magazine *Masses*—which was outstanding in its coverage of art, literature, and socialism—had been charged with sedition. Meanwhile, Dehn and Flanagan talked about working on a ship bound for China. Gág felt left out of their plans and was peeved by "the unevenness of the sexes" (Diary 36, 16 December 1919).

As part of one plan to earn an income, Gág and Dehn launched a business to make designer batik dresses and smocks. They used the Malaysian method of placing wax on cloth and dying the material, but the clothing did not sell. She also worked on an art project for Bemis, a Minnesota company with which Schmidt had connections. In November 1919, Gág received several hundred dollars for an advertisement that would appear in *Vogue, Good Housekeeping,* and *Woman's Magazine* for a new soap and dye called "Magic." In 1919 and 1920 Gág worked as a fashion illustrator and drew dance frocks for Schwartz and Ehrenreich. *Broom* and *Liberator* purchased her drawings for reproduction beginning in 1921. By then she had a salaried job in New York City that she didn't dare forfeit by taking a long vacation to Minnesota. She visited in New England instead and enjoyed the city, as men invited her to the theater and to restaurants. A bookseller whom she called her "Dance Man" arranged to meet her at ballrooms on a regular basis and occasionally took her to dinner.

As for her art work, Gág succeeded in commercial fashion illustration, working both full-time and on a free-lance basis. She earned good money drawing fashion illustrations and soap advertisements and designing pamphlets. She dreamed about travel to Germany and France to see the art and the landscape and asked her friend Harold A. Larrabee how much it would cost to spend a year in Europe,[10] but decided against the trip in favor of saving money, with her still needy siblings in mind. During that time, she also refined her "standard of ethics," writing to Schmidt, "What's good for my art is good and the opposite is bad. I STILL FEEL THAT THE BIG THING IS TO BE MYSELF." In the same letter she added, "I cannot bear to be placed below men," with whom she preferred to be "shoulder to shoulder" (Gág to Schmidt, 18 July 1921).

An enterprise named Happiwork Company seemed promising at the outset. The corporation planned to manufacture toys, papers, and cut-outs for preschool- and kindergarten-age children. On 23 June 1921, five people signed the Happiwork contract in Branchville, Connecticut. Designated as artist, Gág's most innovative creation was a flat illustrated cut-out that could be folded into three dimensions. By rotating the box, one could read a story, such as "The House that Jack Built." This venture gave her not only a chance for work but also to spend weekends in the country. In rural Connecticut, she sketched and painted, but also told stories to two preschoolers who were in the same household, the children of Happiwork employees. Gág began a "Notebook of Ideas" for stories, listing possible titles such as "Alice in Blunderland," "Bobo," "The Funny Thing," and "Snippy and Snappy." She wrote down titles for "Unnatural History" plays-on-words, such as "The Horse Radish," "Tiger Lily" and "Fountain Penguin."[11] Then she mailed drafts of three stories to Minneapolis for her sister Dehli to type. These were "Millions of Cats," "The Funny Thing," and "Snippy and the Mop."

Gág took the typed manuscripts to several New York publishers, "but as no interest was shown in them, they went into my 'Rejection Box' along with many other lost hopes," she wrote later.[12] Despite the rejections, perhaps in part because she neglected to show the sketches accompanying the text, several of these stories led to books later.

In October 1921, Adolf Dehn left for Europe with the understanding that Gág would join him when she completed more material for Happiwork. She immediately developed an intimate relationship with Humphreys. Gág continually postponed her travel plans for Europe. Instead, she traveled with Humphreys in the Midwest, but returned alone to Minnesota. Known for his wit and sense of humor, Humphreys also supported Gág in her work. A cum laude graduate of the University of Pennsylvania, he received a monthly stipend from a family inheritance and was therefore somewhat financially independent. Raised as a Baptist in Philadelphia, Humphreys now called himself an atheist. As an insight to his character, while at military camp Humphreys refused to comply with rules about wearing identification "dog tags" and got into considerable trouble.

Gág's close relationship with Humphreys was fraught with a problem: his occasional heavy drinking, which Gág could barely tolerate, as it brought to mind her mother's condition and her memories of those young adult days when "things went crooked" (Diary 44, 25 August 1928). She commented in 1931, "I am so terribly fond of Earle. I don't want us ever to be separated and yet sometimes I wonder" (Diary 50, 30 January 1931). Humphreys was not her only male friend; she was fond of others, and was generally not happy without a man around. Nonetheless, Humphreys is the man Gág would eventually marry.

During these years, Gág created enough drawings to be ready for a one-person show from 15 February to 1 April 1923 at the Ninety-Sixth Street Branch of the New York Public Library. For the first time since arriving in New York City, Wanda Gág received attention in the press. A newspaper critic commented on the humor in her landscapes and interiors. One drawing incorporated a steep slope, unfenced cows, and tall grass with a sign, "Farm for Sale." Additional recognition came when the May issue of *Pioneer* magazine reproduced several of her works, such as "Sea Chest," "Landscape," "Connecticut," and "Interior."[13]

With money in her pocket from her more profitable commercial enterprises, Gág decided to leave New York City for at least a season to draw and paint. Following her exhibition at the New York Public Library in 1923, she resigned from her commercial art assignments in New York City and moved to Connecticut. "I'm going to draw what I like, even if *nobody* else likes it" (Gág to Scott, 16 January 1944, MHS). She experimented with painting on sandpaper, her own innovation. At this time in her career, she could not afford to buy lithograph equipment, which she had used in art school. Instead, she made a few prints from lithograph crayon drawn on sandpaper instead of on the usual stone or metal.

While Gág found satisfaction in drawing and painting what she pleased, she coped with disappointments in other aspects of her life. Gág temporarily lost the funds she had invested when the Happiwork Company failed, and Adolf Dehn had fallen in love with a ballerina while in Europe. Gág postponed her international plans once again, and in fact never left the United States of America. She would later comment that her prints and books traveled for her.

Gág spent summers with Humphreys, enjoying together the "rambly up and downy land, honest to goodness Connecticut topography. I don't have to go outside of my rent-limits to draw or paint. There is enough material in these 17 acres for years" (Gág to Larrabee, 23 October 1924, CLRC). Gág was determined to preserve her privacy. She was pleased that for four months she had kept secret from her neighbors the fact that she was an artist. "I have always been fond of running much of my life on a mysterious or secret basis because in this way no one knows what kind of work I am doing" (Gág to Larrabee, 21 October 1924, CLRC). She prevented gossip by purchasing a Woolworth wedding ring to wear on occasion. During this time, Gág rephrased her motto: "What's good for my work is good, and anything that hampers it is bad" (Gág to Larrabee, 24 September 1923, CLRC).

While she created art in the country, Gág needed to exhibit and sell her art in the city. With artist William Gropper, five years her junior,

Gág collaborated on a newspaper want ad, a publishing enterprise, and the joint opening of their forthcoming exhibits. The ad in the *New York World* read, "YOUNG ARTIST whose work is acclaimed to be contribution to the period wishes to be relieved of financial worry during year in return for large portion of best work done during that time." Gág later glued the want ad into her "Blaa Book" and added a pencil notation, "We hoped *one* of us would get something out of it. No go!"[14]

Gág and Gropper founded in 1924 an editorless magazine, entitled *Folio.* The concept was that each writer or artist in the cooperative was responsible for one or both sides of a single page to be placed in the portfolio. It would be printed as is, with "no editor, no policy." The only censor would be the U.S. Post Office. They planned for October as the publication date. A limited edition of only 1,000 copies would be printed, and each copy would cost $10. Countee P. Cullen (an important poet in the Harlem Renaissance), Jack Lewis, Allen Tate, Gropper, and Gág were among the contributors. Only one issue was printed: volume 1, number 1. In spring 1924, Gropper and Gág announced openings of their shows at the same library branch where Gág had exhibited the previous year.

Then for several seasons from 1925 through 1929, Gág rented a house on Buffalo Hill Road near Glen Gardner, New Jersey. She remarked in a letter that country living "gives me a standard of simplicity, and a delight in things usually considered ordinary" (Gág to Larrabee, 23 August 1926, CLRC). The house she named Tumble Timbers was on a three-acre farm with space for a garden. Gardening was so important to her that she recorded each prospective vegetable or flower in her correspondence or her diary. One season she planted seeds for nineteen different vegetables, morning-glories, and zinnias. Gág asked the owners, whom she paid $8 a month, to refrain from repairing the sagging porch roof. She found the resulting design intriguing. Inside, too, the oiled-paper lamp shades cast curious light and shadow on the household furniture. She might have continued renting longer, but neighbors built a house too close for her comfort. Highly productive during these months, Gág not only drew and painted but made lithographs and linoleum cuts. She painted the vegetables and flowers she had planted as they matured. Gág spent her winter months drawing interiors in her New York City apartment.

Humphreys tried to market Gág's projects. Her earlier, failed venture with Adolf Dehn to make and sell batik smocks emerged in a new form—a publication. Humphreys found a buyer for her instructions, proposed cover design, and twenty-one illustrations on making batiks. The *Woman's Home Companion* purchased the three proposed articles for

$250 and published them as a pamphlet entitled *Batiking at Home: A Handbook for Beginners.*[15] When Humphreys tried to sell Gág's "Alice in Blunderland" for the "Jolly Juniors" page in the woman's magazine, however, the editor rejected the proposal.

He succeeded in getting a contract for a year with Premier Syndicate, a William Randolph Hearst enterprise. An advertisement announced "The Cross-Word Fairies with the Wonderland Story Puzzles by Wanda Gág" for Sunday newspapers. Each crossword puzzle was accompanied by a story and an illustration. Italicized words in the story matched the phrase for the puzzle and the completed puzzle made a pattern, such as a cross or a flower. But only a few newspapers subscribed and Hearst lost interest. Humphreys then submitted the unused puzzle stories to *St. Nicholas Magazine,* which published three of the ten "worst and good-goodiest" (Gág to Larrabee, 31 March 1925, CLRC), in Gág's estimation. They appeared in the March, April, and May issues in 1925. Gág concluded that "Americans are not really interested in going out of their way where the intellects of their children are concerned" (Gág to Larrabee, 31 March 1925, CLRC). *John Martin's Book* accepted Gág's crossword puzzle story, but decided to find another illustrator to create a drawing to accompany the puzzle.

Among publishers, Humphreys contacted Milton Bradley, Jonathan Cape and Harrison Smith, George Doran, and Alfred A. Knopf; he even tried a manufacturing enterprise, Proctor and Gamble. The proposals differed, but all the prospective clients responded negatively. Louise Seaman, who was the first children's book editor in the United States and had moved from Doubleday to Macmillan, replied that she had seen Gág's work several years before and was still uninterested. Simon and Schuster's reason for rejection was that it already published a substantial crossword puzzle list. Humphreys then described to Marcus A. Heyman an idea for "Fairy Soap" advertisements, incorporating a floating cake of Fairy Soap, Grime Suds, and other ideas. To Frederick Stokes, he proposed "Funny Fairy Tales." While Humphreys pursued these many ventures to cover living expenses, Gág worked on her art.

Success as an Artist

The year 1926 was a watershed for Gág, due in large measure to her show at Weyhe Gallery. Located on Lexington Avenue in New York City, the gallery was known for the discovery of important new artists, especially printmakers. It became Gág's primary showcase. Carl Zigrosser, who served as the director from 1919 to 1940, was Gág's critic and intimate friend. Egmont Arens, who accompanied Zigrosser to Tumble Timbers to select art for the forthcoming show, remarked that he had already seen imitations of her work. He nicknamed the copies as belonging to "The Tired Bed School of Art."

Her Weyhe Gallery Show in November—containing drawings, lithographs, and watercolors—introduced to the public her experimental medium of watercolor on sandpaper. This innovative technique lent a scintillating dimension to the subjects. Tumble Timbers appeared on the catalog cover, and Rockwell Kent wrote the introduction. The show called the art community's attention to Wanda Gág. As a result of sales, she could afford to continue to rent Tumble Timbers. With payments from *Woman's Home Companion* and the Weyhe Gallery sales, and the possibility of borrowing from her sister Nelda, Gág had six months of freedom from "commercial agonies," during which she contributed art to the avant-garde *New Masses* (launched the previous May) in six issues from May to December.

An anonymous essay by Gág appeared in the 22 June 1927 issue of the *Nation*.[16] Entitled "A Hotbed of Feminists," it was the seventeenth and last contribution in a series entitled "These Modern Women." Writing under the pseudonym "Senta Muhr," she thought she camouflaged her family and hometown. She referred to the town as a "mediocre Middle Western village" (*Nation,* 691), named her sisters Barbara and Erda, and her beau Homer. In her description of her artist father and his family, however, there were revealing details. Both parents differed from the neighbors in their artistic, economic, and religious outlook. The father of many girls awaited a son. When the parents died, the siblings stayed together rather than accepting adoption, guided by the eldest's "plan." Acquaintances unexpectedly identified the author as Gág, who "never thought *Nation* would penetrate the depths of New Ulm" (Gág to Larrabee, 21 August 1927, CLRC).

After the 1926 exhibit at the Weyhe Gallery, recognition came more readily to Gág in the fine art community. Gág's art appeared in the best museum shows and in competitive exhibitions for printmakers. The American Institute of Graphic Arts selected Gág's "Elevated Station" for the "Fifty Prints of the Year," the first of several honored. In addition, her work appeared in numerous exhibits. One of the first exhibits outside the New York area was at the Minneapolis Institute of Arts, "Drawings and Watercolor Show by Wanda Gág, Adolf Dehn, and Richard Lahey," which featured the two former students and an instructor. She also exhibited at the American Print Makers Society shows from 1927 through 1936.

In 1930, the Print Club of Philadelphia gave Gág the first prize for the American Lithography Annual Exhibit for "Lamplight." The Denver Artists' Guild gave her an honorable mention in its 1934 Group Exhibit. In addition, the Metropolitan Museum of Art in New York, where she spent hundreds of hours as a student and as an attendee at exhibits, selected a print of "Lamplight" for purchase in the Artists for Victory show in 1942. In 1944, the Library of Congress in Washington, D.C., chose "Barns at Glen Gardner" as its purchase prize. The Boston Museum of Fine Arts, the Art Institute of Chicago, the Cleveland Museum of Art, the South Kensington Museum in London, the Bibliothèque Nationale in Paris, the Kupferstich Kabinett in Berlin, and other prestigious museums purchased her work for their permanent collections.

In 1943, the Metropolitan Museum of Art requested drawings and prints for a "Cats in Art" exhibit, to which Gág submitted "Siesta," "Winter Garden," and "Cats at the Window." Over the years, cats as a subject gained prominence in Gág's fine art projects. From the first sale of *Millions of Cats* in 1928,[17] her publisher, Coward-McCann, and the public associated Wanda Gág with cats. Gág discussed with Coward-McCann staff the possibility of a book of her cat drawings in the late 1930s, which did not materialize. She drew cats in many positions; three peer out for the wood engraving "Cats at the Window" (1929). One sleeps on the couch in the lithograph "Grandma's Kitchen" (1931). She brought her cat with her on a visit and made a lithograph on stone, "Snoopy in Lewis Gannett's Garden" (1932–33). Two appear in another, "Cats and Flowers" or "Winter Garden" (1935). "Siesta" (1938), a lithograph selected for the New York World's Fair exhibition "American Art Today" based on models in *Millions of Cats* but with seven cats napping as the subject, suggested that Gág had many cats; actually, she owned only one or two cats at a time. Her cats Snoopy and Snooky, acquired in 1928 while she was working on *Millions of Cats,* lived until 1933 and 1935, respectively.[18] Nuppins and Liesl arrived in the mid-1930s. Gág also had a dog named Purple, who was jealous of the kittens.

Gág held a cat in one of her favorite photographs, taken by brother-in-law Robert Janssen. Collectors of cat books wrote to her; she received invitations to cat shows (such as the Big Cat Show at the Hotel Pennsylvania in New York City) and was asked to intervene in animal rescue projects.

By 1928 Gág was well connected to both galleries and people in the New York City art circle. Artist Rockwell Kent and Zigrosser were her champions. Gág met photographer Alfred Stieglitz at an exhibit at the Weyhe Gallery in 1926. She became acquainted with Stieglitz's wife, artist Georgia O'Keeffe, in January 1928 at O'Keeffe's exhibit at Stieg-litz's Intimate Gallery. Gág saw her again when both were invited to exhibit at the National Academy (Gág to Larrabee, 16 January 1928, CLRC). O'Keeffe was as excited about the Southwest as Gág was about springtime. Gág annually planned "to snatch a little of the spring land-scape before it descends from its height" (Gág to Larrabee, 9 May 1928, CLRC). O'Keeffe and Stieglitz invited Gág for dinner in New York City and later with Zigrosser for a weekend at Lake George in the fall. They urged Gág to extend the time for more than a week to get a good rest. For Gág, however, there was little time to relax. Not only did she contend with her own yearning to draw, but there were requests from the art com-munity. As a result of her growing fame, Gág gave a lecture to the Art Students League at the Metropolitan Museum of Art on 14 February 1931 to be followed the next week by one at the Brooklyn Museum of Art.

Journalists, too, found Gág personally engaging. Several interviewed her before and after the Weyhe show. Marya Mannes highlighted her as an "individualist" in the new journal *Creative Art*[19] and selected several of Gág's works for reproduction: the linoleum cut "Departure" for the title page; a watercolor, "The Red Barn," in full color opposite Rockwell Kent's editorial. Ann Herendeen captured another aspect of Gág's per-sonality in a *Century* feature, "Wanda Gág, The True Story of a Dynamic Young Artist Who Won't Be Organized."[20]

Gág's appearance as well as her art intrigued people. "She is a small vivacious person, in her first thirties, but looking as if she were in her first twenties. She is dark, short-haired, with a straight bang across the forehead, and beneath it quick, merry eyes and quick, merry lips."[21] Gág loved clothing, and in both correspondence and diaries she described the dresses she wore for events. "New York is a wicked city in the spring and fall. On all sides of me are the most worldly, material temptations in the form of gowns, jackquettes, shoes, silk stockings, dress materials. . . . It requires a constant and stern inner discipline . . . to resist them. . . . Europe or this skirt? . . . oil-paints or this dress? . . . This jackquette or a round trip to Connecticut?" (Gág to Larrabee, undated, probably spring 1923, CLRC).

Despite her fondness of New York City's art community, Gág believed that the quiet seclusion of the country would be more conducive to the concentration necessary to creative work. Fixing up a rented country home and, after June 1931, her own rural farm demanded so much time and effort, however, that Gág's drawing activities sometimes suffered. Moreover, Gág turned to books, both adult and children's, which seem-ingly removed her further from fine art.

Success as an Illustrator

Before creating her first children's book, Gág illustrated two books for adults while in New York City. In 1927, a fine press printed 195 copies of Spencer Kellogg's *The Autumn Embers*[22] and 295 copies of *The Oak by Waters of Rowan,*[23] both illustrated by Gág. Unfortunately, the relationship between Kellogg and Gág soured over a fee. Since the early 1920s, when the business venture Happiwork had collapsed and Gág had lost money, she referred discussion of finances to Zigrosser and later to Humphreys. Kellogg considered Gág's fee of $100 to illustrate his poetry too high, suggesting $65 as fair. She asked Zigrosser to intervene on her behalf as "It has always been a torture to me to be my own business manager. . . . Please forgive me, then, for not being able to talk business" (Gág to Kellogg, 23 January 1927, CLRC). Zigrosser supported her, noting the "vast difference to an artist between doing a commission with someone else's idea and doing what he or she really wants to do" (Zigrosser to Kellogg, 21 January 1927, CLRC).

The year 1928 was fortuitous for Wanda Gág. At her one-person show in the spring at the Weyhe Gallery, a brand new editor, Ernestine Evans, at a brand new company, Coward-McCann, requested an appointment and asked Gág to make a children's book. The result of this happy event was *Millions of Cats,* which launched Gág into a field that gave her multiple benefits. The book provided her with a steady income from royalties during the forthcoming Great Depression and brought her popularity and fame. It also gave her opportunity to travel for book promotions, with occasional visits to her hometown of New Ulm.

Following her debut with *Millions of Cats* in the children's book field, Gág wrote and illustrated other picture books—*The Funny Thing,*[24] *Snippy and Snappy,*[25] *The ABC Bunny,*[26] *Gone Is Gone,*[27] and *Nothing at All.*[28] She also translated and illustrated the Brothers Grimm fairy tales, which materialized as *Tales from Grimm,*[29] *Snow White and the Seven Dwarfs,*[30] *Three Gay Tales from Grimm,*[31] and *More Tales from Grimm,*[32] all published by Coward-McCann.

Not only did Gág complete her first children's book in 1928, but she worked on six linoleum blocks commissioned by Spiral Press for the next year's calendar. Her drawings instill energy into the equipment then used for printing a book—type cabinet, platen press, type frames, paper cutter, rotary press, and book case. Two years after illustrating *Autumn Embers* and *Oak by Waters of Rowan* and one year following the successful *Millions of Cats,* Gág illustrated another book for adults, Michael

Wigglesworth's poem *The Day of Doom.*[33] An American colonial period poem from the seventeenth century about the Last Judgment, this book was one in a series of fine reprints from American literature. Joseph Blumenthal from Spiral Press hand-picked Gág as the illustrator after viewing her work at the Weyhe Gallery. On commissioning her, he even offered to send her a book with New England gravestone art. Her final illustrations included a skeleton holding a scythe, winged angels with trumpets, men in hell, and flowers. Spiral Press printed 535 copies, and Random House distributed them.

Humphreys now represented Gág in financial deliberations. That made her publisher Thomas Coward remark much later: "In eighteen years of close association, I have never known Wanda Gág to ask about, much less to complain about the sales, the advertising, the promotion, or the distribution of any of her books."[34]

From 1932 to 1935 her efforts with illustration took precedence over her fine art drawing. Unfortunately, two illustration projects she considered never materialized—James Stephens's fantasy, *The Crock of Gold* (1912), and Henry David Thoreau's *Walden.* Humphreys drove her to Walden Pond in Concord, Massachusetts, where she sketched on site. After completing two drawings, she worked with printer Joseph Blumenthal. In discussing her selection of type, she admitted that she didn't know specific names, but wanted a "round airy" typeface. She hoped that Limited Editions Club would publish it, but then discovered that the company's selection policy excluded popular reprints. Gág felt that the beautiful writing of Thoreau's *Walden* should reach more people. To a friend, she expressed her regretful resignation from the project concluding, "I don't want to be a party to '. . . Snobpublishers'" (Gág to Edith Newton, 18 November 1932, CLRC).

Children's books kept Gág from financial disaster during the Depression. This is evident in her own words quoted from her Guggenheim Fellowship application in 1939: "When the depression put works of art, especially paintings, into the class of luxuries, I had to turn my efforts to something more saleable, and in my case this happened to be juvenile books."[35] She was loyal to her publisher through good times and bad, and Coward-McCann was loyal to Wanda Gág. Thomas R. Coward lauded Gág, who "could not be hurried. The result was a singular perfection of output which suited her spirit" (Coward, 2). Despite the difficult times following the stock market crash and Depression, Gág persevered and Coward-McCann responded to the difficult economic situation by sharing space with another publisher and finding a distributor to handle sales. Putnam Publishing Company's corporate structure took over Coward-McCann at this time, but allowed the company to keep its identity and name.

These same children's books, however, took precious time away from Gág's first love, drawing and painting. In the late 1920s she spent time studying the "Chemistry of Paint" and yearned for time and opportunity to pursue her fine art. Continuity in her drawing and painting was Gág's goal throughout her adult life, but life's matters had a way of interrupting her commitment. Deadlines dictated by publishers were correlated to income. Gág also contributed drawings to both adult and children's magazines. Among the adult magazines that published her illustrations were *Broom* (1921), *New Masses* (1926–28, 1931, 1936), *Theatre Guild Magazine* (1928–29), and *Wings* (1938). Stories with crossword puzzles appeared in *St. Nicholas* and *John Martin's Book*. The *Horn Book Magazine* published an essay, and she wrote and illustrated an autobiographical article, "I Wanted to Draw," for *Story Parade*. Gág recalled her surprise when as a child she became aware that people in general did not know how to sketch with a pencil. She reiterated her father's advice to draw what was nearby: "Almost anything is beautiful and 'drawable' if you can only look at it in the right way," she wrote.[36]

Although Gág wanted to make her reputation in fine arts, the sales of her children's books sustained her financially. She was guaranteed $1,000 per year from royalties and felt confident she would succeed in finding another publisher if Coward-McCann folded (Diary 26, July 1938). Other publishers who had earlier rejected Gág's overtures now wooed her. May Massee invited her to work on a book for Viking Press, and Helen Dean Fish suggested a book for J. B. Lippincott.

Gág stated consistently that she maintained as high a standard in her children's books as in her fine art. She also realized that she had a good reputation in the children's book field. "In the juvenile field, I may now, I suppose, just bragging, consider myself at the top" (Diary 26, July 1938).

Other Ventures

During the Depression especially, Gág's artist friends struggled financially. Some created picture books while others involved themselves in designing greeting cards. Printmaker Lynd Ward began illustrating books in 1928. Three of these books were published that year, including Dorothy Rowe's *The Begging Deer, and Other Stories of Japanese Children*.[37] Ward then created woodcut illustrations for novels, including *God's*

Man.[38] Rockwell Kent wrote and illustrated *Wilderness*[39] and *N by E,*[40] among others. Fritz Eichenberg, an American born in Germany, also illustrated children's books in the 1930s and 1940s, including at least one job offered to Gág earlier. Gág's publisher, Coward-McCann, produced George Biddle's *Green Island.* Both Ward and Eichenberg reviewed Gág's books.

In the mid-1930s the American Artists Group, of which Gág was a member, printed holiday cards reduced in size from prints and then sold in quantity. Thus they became affordable by the general public. Gág's liberal leanings responded to such a venture. One purpose was to offer fine art at "dime store prices." The participants hoped that the pioneering effort would result in the public buying limited editions of the prints themselves.

Although Gág considered herself at the top of the children's book field, at this juncture in life her perception of herself as a fine artist suffered. By the late 1930s Gág felt that she was going through a rather stale period. Zigrosser encouraged her to move back to New York City and visit art galleries and socialize with other artists. Her memories of life there and in New Ulm were fraught with such financial insecurity and material discomfort, however, that she now preferred her New Jersey rural home. Creating books satisfied her only in part. For a decade, Wanda Gág yearned to engage in more fine art projects. As a result she applied in 1939 for a Guggenheim Fellowship to pursue a renewed interest in oil painting.

Letters of reference provide insight into Gág's professional circle. First, she selected newspaperman Lewis Gannett, who had reviewed her books favorably in his column "Books and Things" for the *New York Herald Tribune* and was a close personal friend. Second, she asked artist Rockwell Kent, who had lauded her work in the Weyhe Exhibit in 1926. Next was Lewis Mumford, the writer and social critic who edited *Dial.* Fourth, she asked Zigrosser, who soon would become the curator of prints at the Philadelphia Museum of Art. Others were E. W. Root and Carl Van Doren. Both Zigrosser and Dehn received Guggenheim fellowships, but Gág did not. She turned to writing, and spent a month in the fall of 1941 preparing several stories to be read on the radio: *Millions of Cats, The Funny Thing, Nothing at All,* and "Fairy Quints," a book in progress that was never published. She also served on the League of American Writers Radio Committee, which had the aim of upgrading radio programming for children.

With Gág's enhanced reputation came an increased pressure to participate in public forums and philanthropic causes. She volunteered for

selected organizations and charities. Gág retained three professional
organizational memberships—American Artists Congress, Author's League
of America, and League of American Writers. When invited to teach a
course in juvenile writing in 1937, however, she declined. She did serve
on the New Jersey and New York state juries for the New York World's
Fair in 1939.

Charities solicited donations from Gág, and she occasionally gave
funds or drawings. The national secretary of the China's Children Fund
asked for permission to place her name among the fund's Committee of
One Thousand, and she granted it (J. Calvitt Clarke to Gág, 27 March
1939, CLRC). She contributed drawings to the China Relief Exhibition
and Sale in March 1939. The cash accumulated was to be forwarded to
China as a "splendid demonstration of international collaboration and
solidarity with the Chinese people." She also permitted the National
Children's Fund of the Junior Red Cross to transcribe *Millions of Cats,
Snippy and Snappy,* and *Gone Is Gone* into braille free of royalties. For its
children's ward, the New York State Psychiatric Institute and Hospital
received permission to reproduce her art from *Tales from Grimm* in mural
form. Likewise, the Minneapolis Public Library created a colorful mural
for its children's room of the donkey, dog, cat, and rooster watching the
five robbers from "The Musicians of Bremen." During World War II
Gág purchased war bonds and donated money and art for various
appeals. She submitted a miniature dummy for *Nothing at All* to sell at
an American Library Association auction in Milwaukee for the war effort.

As individuals representing themselves or causes appealed to Gág,
she turned to her publisher for assistance. Coward-McCann responded
to most letters from Gág fans but forwarded selected letters for Gág's
personal attention. Form letters sufficed for most of the routine
requests Gág received from Coward-McCann. A six-page version
began "A Greeting from Wanda Gág to You: Thank you very much for
your letter and for the interest you have shown in my work." It continued with a sketch of her life, a list of her books, and some hints about
the forthcoming *Nothing at All.* Her brother and sister, but not
Humphreys, are mentioned as living with her. A later version of the
form letter to fans, entitled "A Message from Wanda Gág," was "a
kind of intimate blanket letter" (Diary, 27 September 1941). The substantial letter described her working methods, provided an annotated
booklist, and offered suggestions for those interested in writing and
illustrating.

In some cases Gág composed letters by hand for Flavia Gag, and
occasionally Humphreys, to type out and send to fans. For example, in

advising author Ellis Credle she stated, "Children's books should be written by first class writers, for they are a channel for disseminating ideas (against war, fascism, etc.)" (Gág to Ellis Credle, 22 January and 4 May 1938, CLRC). She also responded to a letter from the young James C. Giblin, who grew up to become an author of nonfiction books and an editor for Clarion Press.

Private Life

Family remained important to Gág, but her ties with the Midwest weakened as her siblings graduated from high school and moved to New York City. The single exception was Stella, who married and remained in the Twin Cities. In 1926, "Two more Gags, Dale Maryland and Flavia Betti Salome have been rescued from the insidious middle-class Minneapolis grip, and are now residing in New York City with Asta Theapolis & Thusnelda Blondine" (Gág to Larrabee, 23 August 1926, CLRC). They lived near John Hay Park and the East River. Her brother, Howard, came to New York in 1927 when he joined a vaudeville team. After Gág's *Millions of Cats* was published, she now stayed on Madison Avenue close to the Metropolitan Museum of Art. Gag family members gathered for Christmas tree decorating and exchanged 10-cent gifts. Wanda and Flavia Gag both received the inevitable blank books, which could be used for diaries.

In these diaries and with family members and a few friends, Wanda Gág was candid; with others, she chose to guard her privacy. She communicated to a Minnesota friend, "I am pretty much a recluse, and I don't get around much" (Gág to Tyler McWhorter, 5 November 1926, CLRC). From Tumble Timbers, she wrote to a couple, "I will give my real and secret address . . . please never use anything as public as a postal [card] in writing me here. . . . I am especially anxious to keep my affairs to myself and our mail carrier is apt to be snoopy!" (Gág to Larrabee, 21 August 1927, CLRC). Following the publication of her first successful children's book, she became even more adamant about protecting her time and privacy. She chose remote locations to live and work. Moreover, she needed her own space. For serious work she used a shack at Tumble Timbers or a studio at All Creation as a retreat within a retreat.

Gág concluded that she would work on a children's book only during alternate years and that 1930 would be a nonbook year. Furthermore, she decided to look for rural property to buy. The success that followed the publication of *Millions of Cats* and *The Funny Thing* provided funds to purchase land, guaranteeing more privacy. "You have no idea how I am

being hounded by old 'friends,' school-mates, and also new people whom
I never met. So please do not give either my telephone number or my
address to anyone. . . . After all I'm only one person and can't see every-
body" (Gág to Newton, 25 December 1928, CLRC).

From 1920 to 1928 Gág kept an apartment at 527 East 78th Street
in New York City, sharing it initially with friends. From December 1928
to the summer of 1931, she lived at 1061 Madison Avenue; her sister
Dehli and husband occupied the apartment the next two years. Gág preferred country living to the city and sought rural settings during the
summer. In 1921 she spent winter holidays at Tophole near Ridgefield,
Connecticut, and returned to the area during the following summers.
She rented the Chidlow Place nearby and Tumble Timbers near Glen
Gardner, New Jersey, during later summers. Rent approximated $48 per
year, and she used the New York City apartment only in the winter
months. During the summer of 1930, she stayed at Cream Hill in West
Cornwall, Connecticut, and moved to New Jersey in the fall.

In 1931 Gág and Humphreys negotiated on the $3,000 asking price
for a farm near Milford, New Jersey. When she named her studio built
the next year on the property All Creation, family and friends referred to
the entire farm that way. The situation provided Gág with the privacy
she craved. In 1937 she was disturbed by a rumor that a park might be
established close to her country property, but it did not materialize.

To preserve her time for work, Gág increasingly retreated from main-
stream New York society life. Even protecting her time for creative
activity demanded creativity. To maintain privacy while in New York
City, she acquired a private telephone number, used Coward-McCann for
her professional address, and asked her friends and family to keep her
address a secret. She could not remain in the country during the bitterly
cold winters. The coal furnace was insufficient to keep the rural homes in
Connecticut or New Jersey warm and comfortable, and winter blizzards
occasionally prevented mail and coal delivery. During the post-Christmas
months, Gág moved to an apartment or a room in the city where she
attended art shows, met with her publisher, and frequented the public
library. Gág considered large dinner parties a waste of time. She preferred to "take my human beings one at a time" (Gág to Newton, 29
May 1930, CLRC).

She made a virtue of necessity by using transportation difficulties in
rural New Jersey as her excuse for not accepting invitations. Living fourteen miles from a railroad station was always a convenient deterrent.
Snow in winter and mud in spring were greater impediments than usual

because Gág did not drive. She depended on others for rides to the train station or into the city. Before having electricity in 1933 and a telephone in 1936, she relied on kerosene lamps and the postal system for communication with family, friends, and her publisher. The only inconvenience seemed to be making several trips to the printer when a book was in progress. She kept in touch with her family, friends, and publishing staff through correspondence. Flavia Gag kept many of her sister's letters, especially after Wanda asked her to. Gág's longest-lasting correspondence was with Alma Schmidt, whose married name was Scott. She also wrote sporadically to a few friends, such as Harold and Doris Larrabee, whom she had met in 1919; Harold taught philosophy at Union College in Schenectady, New York. Gág and Edith Whittlesey Newton, a fellow artist who exhibited at the Weyhe Gallery, corresponded some years after they met in 1927; Ellis Seymour was their mutual friend.

While all of her siblings looked to Wanda as the head of the family, Flavia looked to her as a mother figure. Wanda was fourteen years old when Flavia was born, and she helped raise the baby. In later life, Flavia noted that Wanda was a "sister and mother rolled in one"[41] and lived with her much of the time after coming to the East Coast. For years Wanda claimed Flavia as a dependent on tax forms. In letters to Flavia at her New York address, Gág advised her to use caution while walking at night, to memorize the subway stops, and to avoid getting "fancy" (a code-word for "drunk"). Furthermore, she advised that if a man accompanied her home, they should use a streetcar rather than a taxi. She concluded a cautionary letter, "Well so much for preaching. I don't believe in scare psychology, but I do believe in psychology of awareness. I think New York is really very safe for a girl who knows how to take care of herself" (Gág to Flavia Gag, 12 June 1932, Harm).

Gág encouraged Flavia to write and illustrate children's books with the caveat, "it's taken for granted that you'll have to get some kind of job besides, for that's not a thing which one can depend on" (24 September 1930, Harm). She suggested that Flavia submit books during the years Wanda didn't publish, so she could "wiggle in" to the field. Flavia followed her advice and produced *Sing a Song of Seasons*[42] and illustrated others, such as *The Story of Kattor*,[43] written by Alma Scott under a pseudonym. She also contributed to several children's magazines.

Although children's books commanded attention in Wanda Gág's life, she avoided having children herself. She thought they would detract from her career as an artist. Nevertheless, she invited her niece and nephew along with their mothers to All Creation and sent them "Rainbow Letters," using variously colored pencils. Scott brought her children along in 1944 when she received a University of Minnesota Fellowship in Regional Writing to conduct research and to write a biography about Gág. During the visit, the adults retreated to the studio to discuss the book and the children played elsewhere on the grounds. Gág dedicated several books to children—*The ABC Bunny* and *Three Gay Tales* to her nephew Gary Harm from Minnesota (deleted in recent printings), *Tales from Grimm* to "four readers," *Snow White and the Seven Dwarfs* to Pat and Janey Scott, and *Nothing at All* to her niece Barbara Jean Treat.

World War II took its toll, affecting the entire household at All Creation. Rationing took effect; and, like all other American citizens, Wanda, Flavia, Howard, and Humphreys had only a limited number of ration coupons for gasoline, shoes, and specified foodstuffs. They continued to raise vegetables as they had before the war. Howard registered for the draft, Wanda purchased war bonds, and both Humphreys and Howard worked for the defense industry. The war curtailed Gág's livelihood, too. A paper shortage precluded large initial printings and reprintings of Gág's books.

War was not the only problem Wanda Gág faced. The family's deficient nutrition in their early years in New Ulm undoubtedly affected Gág's health later in life. Even during his productive years, father Anton's income provided little food beyond what the family grew in the garden and the mother gathered in the woods and fields. After Anton's death, the family was destitute; their meager meals often consisted of cornmeal mush or day-old sugar rolls. The Gag siblings suffered through their mother's nine-year bout with alcoholism before her death and knew firsthand about the consequences of drinking. Gág was keenly aware that both her father and mother had died at the age of forty-eight; she lived with a sense of urgency. She frequently worked to the point of exhaustion and complained of various ailments. On occasion she felt exhausted or dizzy. Gág's eyes gave her trouble, which even glasses did not alleviate, and she visited the dentist often. She experimented with curtailing her consumption of coffee and alcohol, the latter even at holiday time. One doctor suggested limiting work hours, taking naps, and eating vegetarian meals. Gág's siblings also had health problems. Nelda became deathly ill in 1936, and it was her oldest sister who contacted a personal friend who was a medical doctor in New York City. He prescribed an experimental drug, sulfa. Following the remarkable recovery, the family members with their respective spouses became even closer. Humphreys was always part of this group, but only they and a few friends knew the truth about Gág's ongoing relationship with him.

Despite Wanda Gág's charade of occasionally wearing a wedding ring to create the impression that she was married, Wanda Gág and Earle M. Humphreys did not marry until 1943. Gág's reasoning was that they lived as if married. In that year she wrote in her diary about an event the public thought had occurred long ago. When Humphreys's job at a machine shop was threatened on the grounds of his "moral turpitude," they decided to marry. Their first plan was to marry in Poughkeepsie, far enough from New York City to avoid publicity; there they completed the necessary preliminary paperwork and blood tests. But they changed the site to New York City. Brother-in-law Robert Janssen signed the marriage certificate as a witness at the ceremony at Central Baptist Church in New York City on 27 August 1943 (Diary, 1943, CLRC).

Illness, Travel, and Death, 1945–1946

In early 1945, Gág admitted that she was ill, and the doctors performing exploratory surgery in late February discovered lung cancer. Gág did not smoke, but Humphreys was a heavy smoker. The three family members with whom doctors consulted—her husband, her brother, and her brother-in-law Robert Janssen—withheld the diagnosis even from her sisters. From then on, Humphreys devoted himself exclusively to caring for her and lost his job in the process. Gág surmised that her condition was "pleurisy," or inflammation of the membranous lining of the lung, resulting from her cold New York City apartment. She underwent X-ray treatments following the exploratory operation on her lungs.

While Gág was ill, Humphreys sought legal advice on her behalf regarding taxes and her will. Deadlines for her forthcoming Brothers Grimm book had to be postponed. During this difficult time she learned that her beloved Uncle Frank from New Ulm had died at more than eighty years of age. By summer she read the first chapter of the biography Alma Scott was writing about her and completed a watercolor worthy of exhibit, "Philodendron Pertusum."

Humphreys and Gág left by car on Christmas Day 1945 for Florida to escape the expected harsh winter of the New York area. Rose Dobbs, Gág's editor at Coward-McCann, offered to contact one of their authors living in Sarasota, Florida. MacKinlay Kantor, whose book was the first that the company had published, might provide some advice about where the couple might stay at a reasonable price.

Dobbs wrote that New York City experienced exceptionally bad weather, from which Gág was spared; the weather in the South, however, was also

far from ideal, with cold and rain. Good news was that Gág's royalties during 1945 amounted to $8,000 (Dobbs to Gág, 9 February 1946, CLRC).
That would help to offset expenses, as finding both reasonable lodging and
restaurants while driving to and in the South was a challenge.

Gág appreciated seeing Virginia's Blue Ridge Mountains, the ever-
greens in South Carolina, and the orange-red earth of Georgia. But she
was anguished by racial segregation, noting towns with separate stores,
schools, and churches for African-Americans. She heard the word "'nig-
gers,' she wrote, "which makes me boil" (Gág to Jane Scott, 9 April
1946, MHS). After staying for a while on the Atlantic Coast of Florida,
they drove to Venice, Fort Myers, and Sarasota on the Gulf of Mexico
before heading home in April. Occasionally she made a rough watercolor
sketch of some appealing scenery; petticoat palms, especially, delighted
her. Work days alternated with an X-ray treatment for Gág or a tennis
game for Humphreys.

The couple arrived back in New York City in late spring and then
went to All Creation in the country. While Humphreys dug up the garden, Wanda stayed in bed, "trying to keep quiet" (Diary, 1 June 1946).
Gág completed a few more final drawings for the Grimm edition. Her
last entry in her diary was 15 June. When she became critically ill, she
went to Doctor's Hospital in New York City and died a few days later,
on 27 June 1946. Her funeral service was private, with only immediate
family present. Wild flowers formed the single floral piece. Following
Gág's cremation, her sister Dehli and husband Robert Janssen scattered
her ashes on the pathway to her studio at All Creation (Janssen to Scott,
16 November 1969, MHS).

Most family members and even close friends had no warning about
the seriousness of Gág's condition. Many learned about her illness and
death from a newspaper. The obituaries noted the dual role she played in
both the fine art and children's book fields. Some commented on the
fairy-tale story of a poor girl from the Midwest who went east to the big
city and became famous. None commented on the remarkable tenacity
and effort required to fulfill her father's expectation that she succeed as
an artist. Colleagues and friends planned exhibits and publications as
memorials, and the next year Coward-McCann published her *More Tales
from Grimm* posthumously.

Gág's siblings were on her mind even at the end of her life, as they
had been when she became the head of the family twenty-nine years earlier. In her will, she divided her property into tenths. While her husband
and the unmarried Flavia and Howard were designated to receive two-

tenths each, the married sisters received one-tenth. The family sold All Creation to artist Clarence Carter, who retained most of the buildings but moved the studio from the top of the hill closer to the house. It still contains the wood-burning stove. The other studio and outhouse remain intact. George Glotzbach photographed the property with the buildings in 1991 and presented copies to the Brown County Historical Society in New Ulm. In 1989 researcher Audur H. Winnan observed, "That part of New Jersey is still rural and amazingly unspoiled," adding that the only major change was the paving of a former dirt road (Winnan to the author, 5 November 1989, CLRC).

Along with all Americans who lived in the first half of the century, Wanda Gág experienced the deprivations of two world wars and the Depression. In addition, she endured the loss of her father at age fifteen and her mother at twenty-four, thereafter being responsible for her six younger siblings. In reality, work substituted for magic in Gág's life. Stalwartly engaged in her work until the end of her life, she stayed in the country trying to perfect her forthcoming Brothers Grimm book until only a few days before succumbing to lung cancer in a New York City hospital. There was no fairy godmother in the German variant of the fairy tale "Cinderella" and no fairy godmother in the author-artist's life. Gág achieved fame that lingers today, fulfilling her father's challenge to become a notable artist. She created 122 prints and ten well-known books for children and young people. Her success in two fields—graphic arts and children's literature—was accomplished by relentless hard work rather than by a fairy's wand.

Chapter Two
Millions of Cats:
The Story behind the Story

During the 1920s, many Americans experienced the good life. It was a creative age, variously termed the "Golden Twenties," the "Jazz Age," and the "Roaring Twenties." The book publishing scene had changed in the ten years since Wanda Gág first visited New York City publishers with her portfolio. Several factors converged in this exciting decade, resulting in an invitation for Gág to create a children's book. First, the market for children's books had increased in bookstores and libraries. American publishers established children's book departments and hired specialist editors, inevitably women, to search for appropriate authors and illustrators. The number of children's book titles increased each year. Editor Ernestine Evans discovered Gág at the Weyhe Gallery art exhibit in 1928 and launched her into the children's book world by the end of the year.

The readiness for children's literature in bookstores and libraries was a primary factor in any book's success. Bookstores and libraries at this time were clustered on the East Coast from Maine to New Jersey. New ones spread west through Pennsylvania and Ohio to Illinois and Wisconsin. The Midwest states of Minnesota, Iowa, and Missouri had bookstores; but California and Texas were slow in developing this business. Many towns in the remaining states lacked both bookstores and libraries, although department stores throughout the country sold children's books.[1] Nineteen libraries across the country—including those in Boston, Brooklyn, Pittsburgh, Cleveland, Detroit, Minneapolis, and San Francisco—opened children's rooms in the 1890s[2] and library schools trained the specialists.

Anne Carroll Moore was an example of this trend. A graduate of Limerick Academy and Bradford Academy in New England, she completed the training program at Brooklyn's Pratt Institute School of Library Science in 1896. Pratt was the first library for which architectural plans included a children's room. "Miss Moore," as everyone called her, was head of the Children's Department at Pratt Institute Free Library from 1896 to 1906 and later superintendent of Work with Children at the New York Public Library from 1906 to 1941. She reviewed books for New York City newspapers and national magazines. Moore began editing a children's literature page for the *New York Herald Tribune* in 1924. Coward-McCann published the latter two of three volumes of her reprinted newspaper reviews in 1928 and 1931 as *The Three Owls*.[3] Moore also occasionally reviewed books for *Atlantic Monthly* and *Commonweal*.

Meanwhile, in Boston, Bertha Mahoney and Elinor Whitney opened a bookshop selling children's books exclusively in 1916. Eight years later they founded the *Horn Book Magazine,* a journal serving as a forum for discussion about children's literature, still based in Boston, for which Moore served on the editorial board. By the end of the second decade of the 1900s, enthusiasm and activity mounted in children's book circles. Frederic Melcher, an editor of the trade journal *Publishers Weekly,* and Frank K. Mathiews, chief Boy Scout Librarian since 1912, founded Children's Book Week in 1919. Louise Seaman became the first full-time children's book editor, appointed in 1919 at Macmillan Publishing House. In 1922 Doubleday Page named May Massee to a similar post; she moved to Viking in 1933. By 1926, at least eleven children's departments existed in trade publishing houses. These departments made an impact on the number and quality of children's books. *Publishers Weekly* recorded the publication of 527 children's books in the United States in 1900. By 1927, the year preceding the appearance of *Millions of Cats,* the number had increased to 738. This total represented 608 new titles and 130 other editions.[4] In 1922 children's librarians of the American Library Association established the Newbery Award in recognition of "the most distinguished contribution to American Literature for Children," popularly referred to as the Pulitzer Prize for children's books. The same library association later inaugurated the Caldecott Medal, presented annually since 1938 for the "most distinguished American picture book for children."

Most important for Wanda Gág was the fact that Thomas R. Coward and James A. McCann founded a publishing company. Coward, a Groton and Yale graduate, had managed the New York office of the Yale University Press for two years and then worked his way up through positions at Bobbs-Merrill Company's New York office to become editor. Meanwhile, McCann had worked at Doubleday, Page, McBride, and Hearst's International Library, and then became sales manager at Bobbs-Merrill. These two men established Coward-McCann Company in New

York City in January 1928. By July MacKinlay Kantor's *Diversey* was out and met with success. They appointed Katherine Ulrich, daughter of Dr. Mabel Ulrich, who owned four bookshops in Minnesota, as their first children's book editor. She resigned almost immediately to become the advisory editor of the Junior Literary Guild and was replaced by Ernestine Evans. The latter brought to her position years of experience as a foreign correspondent in Europe and most recently as editor of the *New Republic*'s children's book supplements.

On a scouting trip, she sought promising books in Berlin, Leipzig, Stockholm, and other European cities. Evans purchased the rights to *The Red Horse*, about a Swedish Christmas toy, written by Elsa Moeschlin-Hammar, a Swede living in Switzerland. Another arrangement brought E. Nesbit's Bastable stories from England to American children.[5] Evans then sought Americans to add to the list of children's books to publish in Coward-McCann's first year. Inspired by Mary Mapes Dodge, the editor of the *St. Nicholas Magazine*, which had its debut in the previous century, Evans intended to approach artists of merit. She would ask them to create something for children.

Wanda Gág's second exhibit at the Weyhe Gallery in March 1928 linked editor Evans with the artist. The artist had selected drawings from her two prior years' production, including "Spinning Wheel," which she chose as the illustration on the exhibit invitation. While viewing the exhibit, Evans requested an appointment to meet Wanda Gág, whose work she recognized from *New Masses*. The editor recalled Gág's "firm young oval face, the slender taut body, the short hair, and deep bangs, the compelling dark eyes."[6] Evans expected to ask Gág to illustrate Ouida's *The Nuremberg Stove*.[7] She asked if Gág had ever written and illustrated stories. Gág, whose "rejection box" contained stories already in manuscript form, promised to bring some to her office.

Together Evans and Gág perused a scrapbook of her drawings and manuscripts for stories. Among the work Gág showed her was the *Minneapolis Journal Junior* "Robby Bobby" series. There was another story about cats that Gág had told to preschoolers Joan Aiken and John Huntington in the spring of 1922, while involved with Happiwork in Connecticut. Gág had written some stories in her spiral notebook and had arranged for her sister Dehli to type them. Evans chose the story about cats and offered Gág a contract with a June deadline. Furthermore, Evans recommended the Englishman William Nicholson's book *Clever Bill*, published by Doubleday in 1927, as a prototype for its format. Gág signed the contract somewhat reluctantly in early April. "It seems every spring—the time of year when I wish least to be taken from my painting—there's something that has to be done" (Diary 44, 10 April 1928). Auspicious timing by the brand-new children's book editor in the fledgling publishing company resulted in Gág's first children's book. Gág knew that if she remained in the city she would be distracted from the book. "I like people, but I can't help being jealous of my working time" (Gág to Newton, 19 September 1928, CLRC), Gág confided to a friend. Gág's charisma and organizational ability inspired her family and friends to assist her in meeting the deadline for the illustrations. She moved to Tumble Timbers in the New Jersey countryside. Her sisters Dehli and Flavia did the housework and prepared meals. From a local farmer's wife, a friend got two kittens that served as models.

Writing *Millions of Cats*

Millions of Cats begins with an elderly couple who long to alleviate their loneliness. The old man consequently sets out to find a cat. He returns home with not one cat, but rather "hundreds of cats, thousands of cats, millions and billions and trillions of cats" (*Millions*). To resolve the difficult situation, he asks which cat is the prettiest: all the cats quarrel and eat each other up, leaving only one who does not participate. Jubilant over the kitten, the couple bring it into their home, where they feed and care for it. The linear plot progresses in the manner of a fairy tale, with a quest and the accomplishment of the mission. The main characters are limited to an elderly couple and one cat, with time and place unspecified. The mood changes from anxiety to calm.

Gág's procedure was first to perfect the text and then to work on the illustrations. She inserted the now familiar sentences: "And he set out over the hills to look for one. He climbed over the sunny hills and he trudged through the cool valleys" (Gág typescript, CLRC). Humphreys proposed on a typed carbon copy that she repeat "Cats here, cats there" as a refrain and include the number "trillions" consistently. Gág took his suggestions. She changed the choice of cats from the initial two white ones to a variety of colors. The last one mentioned possesses the specific details of "brown and yellow stripes like a baby tiger" (*Millions*). She also altered the action at the conclusion of the story. Both husband and wife, rather than the woman alone, bring the kitten inside the house and nurture it together.

The story is simple, but in it one can read something of Gág's intellectual position on feminism and on pacifism. She struggled as a woman

in the art world all her life and was vocal about her feminist leanings.
Eight years before she worked on the book, the Nineteenth Amendment
to the U.S. Constitution had given women the vote. Only a year before,
in 1927, her essay "These Modern Women: A Hotbed of Feminists,"
appeared anonymously in the *Nation*. Gág's sense of humor tempers the
text of *Millions of Cats,* but even in its subtlety, the woman dominates. In
the story, the old woman suggests that a cat might offset the couple's
loneliness. The man follows the woman's bidding. Then a humorous
problem confronts him. There are

> Cats here, cats there,
> Cats and kittens everywhere,
> Hundreds of cats,
> Thousands of cats,
> Millions and billions and trillions of cats." (*Millions*)

Unable to select just one, he chooses them all. It is the woman who real-
izes they can't care for the menagerie he brings home.

Pacifist leanings emerge in the fight scene. Two of the most important
men in Gág's life—Dehn and Humphreys—were conscientious objectors
during World War I. Gág, too, recognized the folly of fighting: the millions of cats fight to the death for the glory of being "the prettiest." The
humble scraggly cat, who has no pretenses, survives to bring happiness
to the lonely pair.

Illustrating *Millions of Cats*

To illustrate the text, Gág departed from current practice in three
areas— the medium, the design, and the printing. First, she chose to
illustrate in black ink rather than in color. Gág reverted to a nineteenth century illustrated magazine technique that she had mastered
while drawing for *New Masses* and creating "Farm Sale" and "Circus"
(Gág to Larrabee, 26 June 1928, CLRC). At that time glossy color
plates dominated picture books imported from Great Britain and
Europe as well as those published in America. From England, the nineteenth-century triad of Randolph Caldecott, Walter Crane, and Kate
Greenaway, along with the twentieth century's Beatrix Potter and
Leslie Brooke, used color. Americans W. W. Denslow and E. Boyd
Smith continued the trend. Charles B. Falls printed in colors from
woodblocks for his *ABC,* a much lauded book published by Doubleday

editor May Massee in 1923. As the second children's book editor in the country, she made her initial mark by introducing Falls and Hungarian immigrant Miska Petersham to the American public. Petersham specialized in flat color, illustrating such books as *The Poppy Seed Cakes* in 1924.

She also initiated use of the "double-page spread," designing two facing pages as one. Panoramic scenes—the man crossing the hills to look for a cat, confronting his wife with the cats following him, and the progression of the growing kitten—work especially well with this innovation. Other illustrations, too, benefit from the concept of the double-page spread. Early in the illustrating of the book, Gág cut and folded blank white paper into a miniature book, only 3⅝ inches high and 5 inches wide. She proceeded to make rough sketches, continuing a line for an inclined hill across both pages or drawing on both sides of the opened booklet with mirror-image circles or rectangles (illustrations for *Millions of Cats,* CLRC). From the onset she had a sense of movement from the left to the right to urge the reader to turn the page. When in motion, the man turns and walks to the right.

Then with lightning pencil sketches she drew the cats in various poses and angles on tracing paper. She planned each illustration carefully, leaving nothing to chance. Where the text described the house, "which had flowers all around it, except where the door was" (*Millions*), she made the image exactly. Each of the cats in the foreground differed from the others. Finally, she used ink on high-quality paper for more than thirty finished illustrations. An engraver reproduced the illustrations on plates for the printer.

The author-illustrator also suggested that hand-lettering be substituted for typeset text. She herself refused to provide the lettering. Gág admitted to having poor handwriting, especially when hurried; furthermore, she had developed a kind of shorthand. She frequently apologized to her correspondents about the illegibility of her writing. Although she tried to teach herself to type, she never achieved sufficient skill to use her typewriter. Her sisters Dehli and Flavia took secretarial courses in high school and were expert typists. The publisher hired a "letterer," but Gág was dissatisfied with his work. She complained that the balance of the lettering, "was so large that it took all the brilliance and delicacy out of my black and white drawings. They said I could have them done over" (Diary 44, 1 August 1928). Gág then recommended that the publisher hire her brother, Howard, for the assignment. Coward-McCann paid him $40, which was cheaper than typesetting. Howard first lettered the text in capitals but later switched to upper and lower case. Gág then incorporated the text into the design of the double-page spread. Walter Crane, an English illustrator influenced by the arts and crafts movement, and especially by William Morris, had used hand-lettered text as part of his design. In 1891–92 he journeyed to Boston, Philadelphia, Chicago, and St. Louis to talk about the movement, but few American children's books followed this pattern. Therefore Gág's books seemed innovative. This decision began a trend for Howard to hand-letter all of Gág's picture books.

Keen observation of both city and country scenes enhanced Gág's illustrations. Her scenes of the very old man with cats on his shoulder, on his head, and in his arms resemble pigeon-feeding in a city park. Gág drew the bulging clouds and the low rounded hills of rural Connecticut and New Jersey, both familiar from her exhibited art. The objects in the interior of the couple's home resemble some of her prints. A dust pan hangs on the wall from a nail. In the final domestic scene, a kerosene table lamp casts light on the household furniture. Reminiscent of the New Ulm Biebl family "Grandma Folks," the contented couple sit in rocking chairs, watching the kitten. Pictures on the wall behind them recall their marriage when young. The lamp casts a shadow over a neatly cut piece of cake and coffee cups. Fortunately, the text calls for peasant dress, because Gág felt she could no longer draw the human form accurately after years of drawing distorted figures for the fashion world. Her commercial artwork did, however, teach her the discipline of meeting deadlines and the method of drawing for reproduction.

During the years before the development of the profession of art editor, the publisher's staff or the artist served in that capacity. Gág designed the entire book herself, from cover to cover, including the end-papers. She completed the illustrations by the end of May and commented in her diary, "they didn't look so bad" (Diary 44, 24 May 1928). Gág's work was not over, however. She had to check the work of both engraver and printer and then assist in book promotion. The artist supervised the printing by examining the page proofs sent to her and by traveling to the printing site the day the presses ran. A perfectionist, she chose to make four trips from rural Glen Gardner, New Jersey, to New York City to monitor the printing stages.

Gág proposed that the publishing company print an ample number of copies on fine quality paper. Coward resisted the idea, stating that it would be too costly. They reached a compromise to make a limited edition of 250 boxed copies, accompanied by an original signed woodcut.

Gág received a 20 percent royalty from sales of the boxed edition, which sold for $12, rather than the standard book price of $1.25. She had worked too hard during the last five years and further exhausted herself while working on the book. One of the several doctors she visited prescribed a strict diet, rest half an hour after breakfast and dinner and an added hour at noon, and alternate painting for two or three days with rest for two days. He advised against drinking coffee and encouraged gardening for relaxation (Gág to Larrabee, 5 June 1928; Gág to Newton, April 1928, CLRC). On 1 August 1928 the diminutive Gág weighed only 87 pounds, a low weight for a woman 5 feet, 3½ inches tall.

Gág thought that she would be finished with her obligations regarding the book by fall. She reported the situation in a letter to artist George Biddle. "I've been very busy with my kid-book, *Millions of Cats* and am still for that matter. I innocently thought that all the launching of my little book would mean, would be the writing and drawing of it, with possibly one trip to town for the purpose of wrangling with the engraver. But I have had to make at least a dozen trips to New York this summer, for interviews, business conferences and what not. In about a week I even have to go to Washington D.C. to be a sort of centerpiece for a display of the *Cats* and to shake hands and autograph copies, or whatever it is one does on such occasions."[8] By late summer she needed to unwind, and the Stieglitz-O'Keeffe invitation to visit Lake George came at a good juncture. She rested and took long walks with O'Keeffe.

Publication, Publicity, and Promotion

The final book was a perfect integrated whole, the result of an author-artist who strove for perfection and integration in herself. *Millions of Cats* finally appeared in bookshops as a thirty-two page book for $1.25 on 9 September 1928. Coward-McCann promoted the book with the same enthusiasm that the company originally had accepted it. The publishers purchased a full-page advertisement in the *New York Herald Tribune* book section, decorating it with four illustrations. Gág launched into book-related activities, including autographing sessions and eleven newspaper interviews. Radio, the new popular communications medium, provided another avenue for advertisement. By the end of the 1920s, half of all American households owned a radio. Therefore, publicity director Harriette Ashbrook scheduled Gág to read her newly published story over the New York City radio station WJZ (Ashbrook to Gág, 18 October

1928, CLRC). Libraries and stores requested original art for display. Moore had a table display at the New York Public Library. Marshall Field's also borrowed an illustration to exhibit.

Newspaper and magazine reviewers consistently lauded the book. The powerful ally Moore predicted, "Wanda Gág has something special to say, something to share, in this first picture book of hers which is so sure of a place among early American children's books of the future." She added that "it is a book of universal interest to children living anywhere in the world."[9] Author Elizabeth Coatsworth asserted in the *Saturday Review of Literature* that the text and illustrations must be seen as a whole, noting that the "pictures are quaint and bold, the cats thoroughly feline."[10]

Evans both edited and reviewed Gág's book, a position that likely compromised her critical objectivity and gave her an unusual opportunity to promote the book. In "This Year's Crop," a review for the *Nation,* she appraised *Millions of Cats* as "Easily the best novel since Cinderella, in that genre" and predicted further that it would "last as long as Grimm or Anders[e]n."[11] The book appeared as the only children's book on "The *Nation's* Honor Role for 1928," along with books by notable authors Stephen Vincent Benet, Mark Van Doren, and Upton Sinclair.[12] Not all readers agreed with the complimentary reviews. An anecdote in Augusta Baker and Ellin Greene's *Storytelling: Art and Technique* relates that one librarian, at least, disapproved of the "violence" in the book. Therefore, when telling the story she changed the episode in which the cats fight and scratch each other to death to their simply arguing and running away.[13]

Despite rave reviews and publicity, *Millions of Cats* attained only runner-up (now termed Honor Book) status for the prestigious Newbery Award.[14] Instead, Eric P. Kelly received the award for *The Trumpeter of Krakow,* published by Macmillan. The secretary's minutes recorded, "The applause that attended the announcement of the winner showed the choice to be heartily endorsed by those present" (Smith, 54). Today, however, *The Trumpeter of Krakow* is among a dozen prize winners "considered lowest in popularity," according to historian Irene Smith (89). Yet the book is kept in print because it received the award, and another edition with new, complimentary illustrations by Polish-American artist Janina Domanska was published by Macmillan in 1966. Not one of the runners-up besides *Millions of Cats* was in print as of 1990. The other five were John Bennett's *Pigtail of Ah Lee Ben Loo* (Longmans), Grace Hallock's *The Boy Who Was* (Dutton), Cornelia Meigs's *Clearing Weather* (Little), Grace

Moon's *Runaway Papoose* (Doubleday), and Elinor Whitney's *Tod of the Fens* (Macmillan). Had the Caldecott Award existed in the late 1920s, *Millions of Cats* surely would have received it. No other picture book published that year, even those in color, merited the prize more. *Millions of Cats,* Gág's most popular book, has remained in print from the day it was published. The second printing ran into some difficulty, with Gág accusing the engraver of tampering with the plate for the cover and calling the resultant color "very red and horrid." After that disaster, Gág supervised most of the reprints. She herself controlled the cover color for the third printing, selecting a more orange-red hue. At one time, Gág considered adding color to the entire book, but she abandoned this idea. An entry in her diary notes that "The Cats" had sold over 10,000 copies in a mere three months (Diary 44, 1 January 1929). By February, the number increased to 15,000. Evans commented, "We began to think of it as the mascot of the firm" (Evans 1947, 4). In the aftermath, the farm woman who contributed the kittens discovered that they were the models for Gág and thought she deserved a profit from the book.

Herschel V. Jones, Gág's "Journal Man" from Minneapolis who helped support her financially when she attended art school, never saw the book because he died in May 1928, before it was published. C. B. Boutell, Coward-McCann's publicity director a decade later, calculated that *Millions of Cats* had sold more than two copies per hour for every business hour that the publisher had been in existence.[15] In 1937, the publisher arranged for a new set of plates to be made from the original drawings for the twelfth printing of "Cats," as Gág called the book. "I got the drawings from my safety box and find they need a lot of cleaning up so I'll stick to that until I've got it ready for the printer" (Gag to Zigrosser, 28 May 1937, VP). Even twenty years later two books from Coward-McCann's first list were not only still in print but continued to sell well; they were *Millions of Cats* and *The Bastable Children*.[16]

Despite Moore's conviction that the book would have international appeal, considerable time passed before it was published in countries other than England. Faber and Faber published the book in Great Britain in late 1929. It was one of 433 new titles in the category "Children's Books and Minor Fiction" published in Great Britain.[17] Still, Coward-McCann staff member Rose Dobbs concluded that sales of the British edition of *Millions of Cats* "did not do as well . . . as they should have" (Dobbs to Gág, 12 September 1931, CLRC). A publisher in Berlin was "interested in principle" in translating and publishing the book (Marion Saunders to Gág, 10 May 1931, CLRC), but nothing came of a

German edition. Translations did appear later in Danish, Dutch, French, Hebrew, Italian, Japanese, and Ukrainian. In some languages the refrain is parallel to English. Over the course of three decades, three Danish publishers produced three different translations—by B. B. Moller in 1948,[18] Anine Rud in 1968,[19] and Nanna Gyldenkaerne in 1987[20]—of the same title, *Millioner af Katte*. There are slight differences in the three versions. While the first is hand lettered in a similar fashion to the American, the second is typeset. In all three translated editions, the words "Hundreder . . . tusinder . . . millioner, billioner, trillioner" are as effective in Danish as in English. Franklin Book Programs, a nonprofit organization for international book development, expanded the translations to African and Asian languages. In 1992 a French edition entitled *Des Chats par Millions* was published. A dark blue border and red buckram spine brighten the appearance. The hand-lettered text keeps the interior true to the appearance of the original.

Wanda Gág's debut with *Millions of Cats* proved important to her career and brought her name to the attention of other publishers. Reviews of her later books inevitably compared them with this first endeavor. Other publishers contacted her, even those who had formerly rejected her work. For example, Louis Untermeyer asked if she would make about twenty pen and ink drawings for his forthcoming book because the setting was German and Gág had that "blend of sentiment and humor so rare in illustration—and so characteristic of your work" (Untermeyer to Gág, 5 May 1929, CLRC). When Gág declined, Harcourt Brace published *Blue Rhine, Black Forest* with Untermeyer's own maps and Louis Weirter's art.[21] Moreover, her success brought recognition to her publisher and advanced the development of American children's books. Thomas Coward reminisced, Gág "is the bellwether of our juvenile list and *Millions of Cats* established it in our first year as publishers as one of quality" (Coward to Humphreys, 19 March 1945, CLRC).

Children's literature critics and historians consistently credit Gág with setting a high standard in both text and art form. Barbara Bader summarizes, "Text, drawing and format together constitute its appeal and its lasting distinction."[22] American publishing historian John Tebbel concludes, "It was one of the notable children's books of the century, making publishing history and reviving the great tradition of line drawing begun in nineteenth century magazines" (Tebbel, 562).

Wanda Gág set in motion the American picture-book movement with her *Millions of Cats*. Her significant contribution was integrating the cover, endpapers, illustrations, and story into a complete whole. Like a fairy tale, the narrative gathers momentum to a peak and then moves quickly to its resolution. *Millions of Cats* continues to be a staple commodity in libraries and bookstores. The book's popularity can be accounted for in several ways. It evokes a high comfort level, as the story line is similar to a traditional fairy tale. Because the illustrations are black and white, it is cheaper to reprint and consequently carries a lower price tag; a paperback edition appeared in the United States in 1977. Americans, living increasingly in urban areas, find the cat an appropriate pet. Kittens have a special appeal, along with the elderly couple who remain active despite their advanced years. Moreover, the book suits the modern spirit, as an enterprising individual solves a problem. The image of the old man followed home by the cats has staying power; readers identify with the man's inability to choose a single cat among the many. Finally, a sense of humor permeates both the text and the pictures. All these factors combine to make *Millions of Cats* a classic.

Chapter Three
Picture Books Sell despite the Depression

Respected artists seek new ventures throughout life, challenging themselves to create images in new ways. Wanda Gág was no exception. When asked why she refrained from drawing more caricatures of machines, such as her popular 1927 and 1928 images of "The Stone Crusher," printed in 1928 and 1929, her response was, "Why should I? I did that because it amused me. Perhaps one day I shall see something else that looks like something else and I shall be amused again. But one cannot laugh and laugh at the same joke" (Herendeen, 432). At this juncture in 1929, she declined five invitations to illustrate books written by others. Moreover, she planned to limit herself to illustrating only one children's book a year, "that being my own—with the possible exception of some classic occasionally, to be selected by myself" (Gág to Newton, 25 February 1929, CLRC). She also endeavored to inject fresh ideas into her children's books. Her five original picture books confirm and uphold this principle.

Her first three picture books—*Millions of Cats, The Funny Thing,* and *Snippy and Snappy*—are identical in shape and medium, but differ substantially in text and illustrations. They shared the same genesis, for Gág had told the stories to six-year-old John and three-year-old Joan while living in rural Connecticut when Gág was part of the Happiworks Company. They were grandchildren of Jean Sherwood Rankin, for whom Gág illustrated *A Child's Book of Folklore* when living in Minneapolis. At the suggestion of someone overhearing her, she later wrote down the stories. She sent the "Handy Note Book" drafts for her sister Dehli to type. The fourth picture book, *The ABC Bunny,* departs significantly in both text and illustrations, while the fifth book reverts in form to the earlier ones.

The Funny Thing

While her editor Ernestine Evans preferred a story Gág submitted about two mice, the author's second favorite to *Millions of Cats* was the one that would be published in 1929 as *The Funny Thing.* The plot is about a man who appeases a creature who eats children's dolls. To the horror of Bobo, the gentle mountain man, the fabulous animal even eats the dolls of good children. The story's title comes from a letter Gág wrote to her childhood friend Alma fourteen years earlier, in which she remarked, "Friends are funny things" (Gág to Schmidt, 4 August 1915, CLRC). As with her previous book, Gág first polished the text and then did the illustrations. "Writing is not easy for me," she wrote. "I believe I've rewritten it at least eight times. I'm determined to build it up just as carefully as I would any drawing" (Gág to Newton, 25 February 1929, CLRC). In an earlier draft, for example, Bobo sold food to the forest creatures, while in the final manuscript he gave it to them. Gág invented a name for the candy-like food—"jumb-jills"—in earlier drafts, and finalized it as "jum-jills." The author also deleted the phrase used in an early draft, "There was no such word in the dictionary" (manuscript for *The Funny Thing,* CLRC), to define further the "aminal" character (*aminal* being another word of Gág's invention).

As early as 1923, Gág had brushed ink on sandpaper and assigned the image a title—"Fantasy." Sometime later she wrote on the reverse side that it was "A drawing made at random which became the germ of the Funny Thing" (study in pencil for *The Funny Thing,* CLRC). Only the illustrations conveyed the "aminal" having a dragonlike appearance. The creature smiled and lacked fearsome qualities. Its behavior resembled that of a dog rolling on the ground. Gág realized that it was based some-what on the antics of her dog Purple.[1] The outdoor country and indoor domestic scenes of Bobo's house suited Gág. She drew from the same inner resources and powers of observation as for her prints, but used subjects children would recognize from their spheres of experience: squirrels, cabbages, and kitchen utensils. Light sources, such as the lamp or the tunnel opening, illuminate appropriate space. Lamps and lamplight casting shadows were a specialty of Gág, as she had painted lampshades for quick money in her early New York City years. In two double-page spreads, the lower saw-tooth border duplicates the aminal's row of points down its back.

As with the text, she agonized over the visual interpretation of the story. Among the preliminary steps were "dummies," hinting at the attention she gave to the double-page spread concept and to possible colors for the cover. Gág discarded preliminary choices of the colors rose, turquoise, and yellow, selecting instead orange, blue, green, and yellow for the printed cover. An explanation to Russell Limbach about how she created "The Forge," one of her lithographs completed in 1932, provides insight into Gág's manner of working. "In my work I do not rely on happy accidents; I know beforehand exactly what I want the final result to be and work consciously toward that goal" (Gág to Limbach, April 1946, CLRC).

On Easter Sunday, she "got about fifteen of the drawings blocked out and it looks as though the book might not take as long as [*Millions of Cats*]. No wonder—such a bunch of cats" (Diary 45, 31 March 1929). She admitted being nervous; the illustrations came slowly and she couldn't gauge time. "After toiling on the cover design all day without success," she wrote to Edith Newton, "I was finally so exasperated that I decided to do something violent" (Gág to Newton, 17 April 1929, CLRC), and scrubbed and oiled the bedroom and dining room floors instead. The cover and interior illustrations required two more months of work. As for *The Funny Thing*, Howard hand-lettered the text with pen and India ink. While his hand work, for which he received $100, was cheaper than typesetting, it was something of a burden for Gág, who monitored his progress and reviewed his work.

Gág agonized over the printing. Coward-McCann wanted to keep the price of the book low and consequently had to find a printer that would charge a reasonable fee. Gág went to Rahway, New Jersey, to visit the printer Quinn and Boden three times in a week, and commented in her diary, "heaven knows what would have happened to the books if I had not been there to avert several calamities." She felt that the book would be of higher quality if it could be printed on good paper. "It just bothers me so to see my fine careful lines come out heavier, and my blacks (which are composed of literally thousands of pen scratches so as to keep them from being flat and heavy) come out either solid or else pale black" (Diary 47, 29 October 1929). She acknowledged that the printer had difficulty getting a rich black when he used thick ink for her thin lines. Despite her health problems, such as toothache, poison ivy rash, and infected tonsils, she examined the printer's proofs carefully. She then folded the book as though sewn, reassuring herself that the two pages of illustrations matched. In the final stages, Gág insisted on traveling to the printer to approve all the plates before the final printing.

This second picture book possesses unity similar to *Millions of Cats*. The yellow and blue colors, zigzag border, and images of Bobo and the imaginary creature on the cover carry over to the endpapers. While the aminal steals dolls on the title page, he sits eating jum-jills on the final page, concluding "The End." Either the old man or the aminal faces to the right on each interior page, encouraging the reader to turn the page.

Coward-McCann set the price of the thirty-two page book at $1.50 and published it in October. Gág thought that the printing superseded the printing job for *Millions of Cats* and moreover heard that many people thought it was a better book. During each fall season, some large department stores in major cities displayed the newly published children's books and arranged for author appearances. To promote *The Funny Thing,* Gág traveled to Chicago, Minneapolis, and Cleveland. Since 1919, the same year that a National Book Week was established, Marshall Field's in Chicago hosted an annual book fair. The store ordered 1,000 copies of her second book when she promised to autograph them. She also told stories at the Chicago Latin School. Publishing company salesmen and taxis were at her disposal. "Coward-McCann gave me a liberal expense account" (Gág to Newton, 22 November 1929, CLRC), she commented.

After autographing at the book section of Powers, a department store in Minneapolis, she made an unannounced visit to her relatives in New Ulm. Following a stopover in Cleveland, she returned to New York City where Lord and Taylor's bought two hundred copies. During this time, a financial crisis hit the country. On "Black Tuesday," 29 October 1929, stock prices plunged, ushering in the Great Depression.

Although *The Funny Thing* received some immediate adulation, its reputation never matched that of *Millions of Cats.* Artist Lynd Ward reviewed her book with enthusiasm, exuding, "If the history of the art of the picture book is ever written the name of this artist will undoubtedly be graven there in large letters, for she, writing her story as well as drawing it, has discovered the richest potentialities of each factor and to the process of integration has brought a wealth of originality. No other books have quite that feeling of the artistic whole."[2] Several reviewers and even the *Index of Twentieth Century Artists*[3] mistakenly referred to the illustrations as woodcuts. Reviewers May Lamberton Becker, Helen Ferris, and O. M. Fuller praised the book. The latter, writing for the *New York World,* named it "one of the most attractive picture books of the season," and added that it is "childlike, and shows both originality of idea and illustration."[4] But Rachel Field—who won the 1930 Newbery Award for *Hitty, Her First Hundred Years,*[5] published the same year as *The Funny Thing*—found the book "grotesque . . . conscious and mannered."[6] Unlike *Millions of Cats, The Funny Thing* did not get an honorable mention from the Newbery selection committee.

The story lacks the repetitive phrases used so successfully in *Millions of Cats.* Instead, Gág repeats single and double words. For example, she uses "aminal" or "animal" eight times, "jum-jills" fourteen times, and "Funny Thing" twenty-five times. In the published book, the aminal resembles a cross between a dog and giraffe, but also has a row of blue points down the back of its body like a dragon. Gág's sensibility and sense of humor express themselves in several aspects of the book. When the man offers certain foods, the creature rejects them by turning his head away, like a child. Bobo then pacifies him by camouflaging the same foods in little balls he names jum-jills. The creature then eats them. Bobo's strategy immobilizes the interloper by filling him with food. At the end, the "Funny Thing" is contented with a sedentary life, his tail wrapped permanently around the mountain and the birds feeding him.

Because Gág wrote skillfully, the story survived in anthologies even without illustrations. While the Newbery Award committee ignored *The Funny Thing,* the American Institute of Graphic Arts named Gág's second children's book one of the "50 Books of 1930." Due in part to the difficulty of translating "aminal," *The Funny Thing* has appeared in few foreign language editions. Even the British publisher Faber and Faber postponed its publication for thirty-three years, until 1962.

Snippy and Snappy

Early in 1930, Evans proposed a "Birthday Book" (a calendar-like book on which the book's owner enters people's names next to their birth date) with twelve drawings for the fall of 1930, offering Gág $1,000. Gág wondered what she needed more—money or time. She realized that in addition to spending two months on the book, she would have to contend with correspondence and trips to the publisher and printer and then promotion. Gág decided against doing it. She surmised that the value of the money would not have matched "this feeling of having been true to myself once more" (Diary 48, March–June 1930). In addition, she resisted Bennett Cerf's invitation to illustrate a "Mother Goose" edition for Random House (Gág to Evans, 20 May 1930, CLRC). (Rockwell Kent, who praised Gág's work exhibited at the Weyhe Gallery, was one of the first to invite her to illustrate another writer's book. In 1930, while working for the New York publisher Covici, Friede, he asked her to illustrate with prints a series of books he had in mind [Kent to Gág, 10 October 1930, CLRC].)

Gág revised her plan to create only one book a year to one book in alternate years. She skipped 1930 and revived her "woodland" book idea

in 1931. But because the Depression affected book sales, Gág wondered
if she should withhold even the proposed book until the economy improved. Moreover, the staff at Coward-McCann had changed. Rose Dobbs
had come to the publisher as Evans's secretary in 1929, after working in
the manufacturing department at Alfred A. Knopf. She served as Thomas
Coward's secretary for a brief time before her promotion to head of the
children's book department in 1930, after Evans left.[7] Dobbs then
became Gág's second editor while she worked on the book that was to
become *Snippy and Snappy,* published in 1931.

Gág had difficulty concentrating on the book, partly because her
emotions interfered with her work. Her struggle involved Humphreys,
who had been her closest companion since Adolf Dehn left for Europe in
the early 1920s. Gág admitted that she had mourned for Dehn himself
for only a week (Diary, 30 May 1926). And now Humphreys, who
unlike Gág preferred the city to the country, had become involved with
another woman. Gág was taken by surprise; this was a breach of
"integrity," which, for her, replaced religion. Humphreys eventually
returned to Gág, but thereafter she referred to him as "the Drifter."

Another distraction was the house she purchased in June. Royalties
from her first two picture books enabled Gág to plan seriously for a
permanent home. She yearned for long periods of concentration that a
country setting could provide. Humphreys scouted for available rural
property. In 1931 Gág purchased the 123-acre farm in the Muscanet-
cong Mountains near Milford, New Jersey, that she would come to call
All Creation. The town was situated in west-central New Jersey along
the Delaware River and inhabited by about a thousand people. The
property had a brook, an orchard, space for a garden, and few snakes.
In addition, there were woods, a bountiful horse-chestnut tree, and a
hilltop unfolding splendid views. At that time there was little traffic
and there were good neighbors. Humphreys and Howard Gag cared
for and improved the rural property. They eventually built a dam in
the Quequacommissicong Creek, which meandered through the property, to provide a swimming-hole. When guests visited, Gág expected
them to create something, ranging from a piece of writing
(Humphreys's avocation) to a wood carving (Howard's) to a floral
arrangement. The house, built one hundred years earlier, had three
fireplaces but lacked a modern heating system and plumbing facilities.
Gág spent that summer and those following with family and friends
working on the house. They coped with an early summer flood and a
beehive in the chimney. Fumigators came and then plasterers, carpen-

ters, and plumbers. Gág scrubbed floors and scraped wallpaper. With
the others, she removed poison ivy and planted a garden. After a couple of summers, Gág bemoaned her lack of time for her first love: "No
drawing! No drawing! No drawing!" (Diary, 10 March–28 September
1932).

Gág did eventually get to work on her third book, initially titling it
"Snippy and the Mop." Carl Zigrosser called her "Snappy Eyes" one
evening (Diary 50, 30 January 1931), and the book title evolved into
Snippy and Snappy. The story begins with Father Mouse reading aloud
from his newspaper about houses with kitchen cupboards containing
cheese—all of which foreshadows the story's turn of events. One day his
son and daughter—Snippy and Snappy—play outside with a ball of
their mother's knitting yarn. A young girl picks it up and unravels it as
she returns to her home. The young mice follow her into the house. The
household objects seem huge and overpowering; the mice are confused
by the unfamiliar surroundings. They mistake the floral rug border for
natural flowers and wonder why the pattern lacks fragrance and why
they can't hide under it. Snappy's mirror-image frightens them both into
running until they enter the kitchen and encounter cheese in a mouse
trap. Father Mouse intervenes at the moment of danger to warn the
youngsters. Then he takes cheese from the cupboard and leads them to
the security of their own mouse home.

Preliminary drafts reveal Gág's struggle with rhyme schemes, such as
"hay-field, play-field, gay-field" and

> They rolled it and rolled it
> they rolled it for hours
> Thru ferns and thru flowers
> Thru vales and thru valleys
> Thru long weedy alleys.

She deleted whole sentences, such as "They were crying as tho their little mousie hearts would break." In the final draft, Mother Mouse no
longer says, "I never did like that color of blue" in dismissing the loss of
the knitting ball. Unfortunately, Gág chose to exclude a sentence from
an earlier version explaining why the mice abandoned the knitting
ball—"Snippy and Snappy were so excited about the cheese they forgot
all about Mother Mouse's big blue knitting ball" (manuscript for *Snippy
and Snappy*, CLRC). That would have clarified the situation, but the final
book lacks this sentence.

The accompanying illustrations proved difficult. As in the early 1920s, Gág enjoyed drawing familiar household objects, giving them dignity and a special energy. She tried three versions of the hayfield, and each trial sketch averaged two days of work. "I'm really quite weary of it," she wrote (Diary 50, 24 February 1931). In preparing the illustrations for the house interior, Gág recalled the feeling of overwhelming space she had had on accompanying her father to New Ulm's Turner Hall, where he painted the backdrops. Mushroom tables and chairs in the mouse home were easier to draw than the furniture in the girl's house, which had to be rendered from the underside, from a mouse's point-of-view. In addition, she needed to study the structure of chairs and lamps. She'd sketched the mice that used to come into her studio at Tumble Timbers and recalled the tiny doll furniture and newspapers she had made for her siblings when they were children. As he had for her two previous books, Howard hand-lettered the text for a $100 fee, but placement of the text was more innovative. Where the drawings curve in a rhythmic manner, the hand-written text parallels them.

As with her two previous books, there is a sense of visual unity. The mice walking to the right on the cover appear in silhouette on the end-papers, sleeping on the title page, and scampering away in the final vignette. The drawings communicate movement and pull the reader forward from page to page. Gág drew slightly wavy walls, giving the structures a liveliness. In one whimsical partial-page illustration, only the tails and back legs show as the mice escape through a crack. More dramatic than *Millions of Cats,* the book is also one-third longer. On some pages the illustrations undulate. For example, when the mice children run up and down the hills, the illustrations convey how "they followed it up, they followed it down."

When the book appeared, the usual reviewers—Anne Thaxter Eaton, Lynd Ward, and Helen Hammett Owen—welcomed it. Anne Carroll Moore compared the drawings and printing job favorably with Gág's first book.[8] Ward complimented Gág on the mice's clothing (they wear vests).[9] Rachel Field considered the illustrations better than those in the first two books—Gág "has not made as many of the queer oyster-shell shaped full-page effects"—and liked the story—which "has an excellent moral about meddling"[10] (that is, the mice had no business in a human house).

In spite of such praise, this book, like *The Funny Thing,* was over-looked by the Newbery Award committee, which in 1932 selected Laura Adams Armer's *Waterless Mountain,* a story with a Chinese setting.[11] Irene Smith concluded almost thirty years later that the winner, along with *The Trumpeter of Krakow* (which had edged out *Millions of Cats*), was among the twelve least popular with children through 1957 (Smith, 90). The committee also named six Honor Books, including those by names familiar in the children's book circle: Dorothy P. Lathrop, Rachel Field, and Mary Gould Davis. Faber and Faber in England made a proposal to publish Gág's third book, but its low offer, which reflected the same poor picture-book sales overseas as in America, was rejected (Dobbs to Gág, 15 September 1931, CLRC).

Wanda Gág's Storybook

Between *Snippy and Snappy* and her next publication, *Wanda Gág's Storybook*, which appeared in 1932, Gág suggested the idea of a sewing book to her sisters. As youngsters they created doll clothes and later their own wardrobes. In 1926, Humphreys submitted Gág's idea for a "Sue Sew and Sew" feature to a company in Cleveland, but the publisher rejected it because of what he called "lack of space" (James W. Dean to Humphreys, 8 March 1926, CLRC). Written and illustrated by Asta, Dehli, and Flavia, the book *Sue Sew and Sew* was published in 1931.[12] It consists of twelve lessons for sewing a wardrobe from chemise to beret for Dolly Sue.

Also during this interim, Thomas R. Coward invited Gág to illustrate a manuscript by Walter D. Edmonds at the urging of the author, whom Coward identified in a penned footnote as "a very successful novelist." In the cover letter he sent along with the story, "Death of Red Peril," Coward reported that Edmonds had offered to split any royalties with Gág (Coward to Gág, 4 May 1932, CLRC). Once again Gág refused on the principle that she illustrated only her own books. Only five days later Coward acknowledged her negative response, writing, "It is well to stick to your own" (Coward to Gág, 9 May 1932, CLRC). The Little Company in Boston published the story in 1934 along with other short stories, centered on the Erie Canal, as *Mostly Canallers*. Edmonds eventually won the Newbery Award for *The Matchlock Gun*, illustrated by Paul Lantz and published by Dodd in 1941.[13] Moreover, he went on to receive the National Book Award in 1976 for *Bert Breen's Barn*. William Gropper, Gág's friend from the 1920s, illustrated Edmonds's *Uncle Ben's Whale*,[14] which was named a *New York Times* Choice of the Best Illustrated Children's Books of the Year in 1955.

In 1932, Coward-McCann also proposed the idea of compiling Gág's first three independently published books. Dobbs challenged Gág with, "What I'm aiming at is as good-looking a book and as *new* looking a book as we can get" (Dobbs to Gág, 1 June 1932, CLRC). For *Wanda Gág's Storybook* Gág drew a new cover, title page, and endpapers, incorporating characters from all three stories.[15] Silhouette images on the cover show the old woman shaking her finger at the man holding cats, Bobo feeding jum-jills to the aminal, and the mice poised to follow the little girl. The title page depicts the aminal and cats near the center, with Snippy and Snappy looking on. Umbrella-like trees laden with fruit shelter them. Processions of clouds, birds, and cats cross the endpapers above the mice and mountain creatures. At the urging of Dobbs, Howard Gag carved an image of "The Funny Thing," which stayed in the editorial office for a while.

A crisis occurred when the Coward-McCann staff couldn't locate some of the original illustrations necessary for reprinting. Missing were a page from *Millions of Cats,* and the cover, endpapers, and a page from *The Funny Thing* (Dobbs to Gág, 1 June 1932, CLRC). The publisher never retrieved the original cover; poor record keeping and a move to new headquarters, which further confused the issue, made it impossible to surmise where it had been loaned for publicity purposes. Marshall Field's returned one illustration. Despite a plea from Dobbs in *Publishers Weekly*[16] announcing the loss, the company never retrieved them all, so Gág redrew them. The loss made her nervous, and she later placed her art and diaries in a bank vault. She put other valuables, including her early art work, in a storage trunk and instructed her family members to rescue it first in case of a fire.

When the 112-page book appeared at the price of $2.75, it had a new design for the jacket, title page, and endpapers. Emma L. Brock, a fellow Minnesotan and reviewer for the "Children's Librarians' Notebook" section of the *Library Journal,* commented positively on the book's "durability," but negatively on the "idea of Wanda Gág in wholesale form. Artistically each book should stand alone."[17]

Brock had a point. Because each of the stories is unrelated to the others, each really deserves its separate covers. Still, the American Booksellers Association selected *Wanda Gág's Storybook* to present to the White House Library (Dobbs to Gág, 12 October 1934, CLRC). After going through a sixth impression in 1939, the book went out of print. Library appropriations across the country were suffering from the Depression, and juvenile book sales diminished.

Meanwhile, Gág asked Carl Zigrosser to negotiate royalties for future books on her behalf with Coward-McCann. She hoped for 12.5–15 percent. She wrote to him, "I do think that Mr. Coward is honest as far

as businessmen go and I do know that the competition with cheap gaudy
books is terrific. I'm perfectly willing to cooperate with them, if they can
convince me that it's wisest" (Gág to Zigrosser, 18 May 1932). Humphreys negotiated for the forthcoming book contract. Coward wrote to
assure Gág that the copyright for any forthcoming book could be in her
name and that she could buy the plates and stock at cost if the company
liquidated. "I should always want to do whatever seemed fair, and nothing, under any circumstances, to your disadvantage from either a personal or commercial point of view" (Coward to Gág, 20 January 1933).

The ABC Bunny

Gág's next book project, following *Snippy and Snappy* by two years, was a
departure from her first three picture books. She studied an entomology
textbook with the thought of producing an insect book, but now she
envisioned an alphabet book with several innovative characteristics.
First, Gág told a story rather than merely depicting objects in an alpha-
betical sequence. Second, she selected a rabbit in its natural surroundings for the subject. Third, she illustrated it with lithographs. Last, she
designed it for a large format.

As usual, Gág produced draft after draft of the text and refrained
from developing complete illustrations until she polished the text. She
listed rhyming words, such as "view, dew, mildew, few, blue, blew, flew,
new." Then she tried tentative phrases, such as "A is for an apple tree"
before settling on "A for apple big and red." For the letter "F" she tested,
"F for Ferns with fringe and frill/Frowning cloud beyond the hills," but
concluded that a frog appealed more than ferns to three- and four-year-
old children. The last letters of an alphabet book often pose problems for
those selecting appropriate words. Gág solved the problem by using "X"
in the word "eXit" and involving the reader in the conclusion—"Y for
You, take one last look, Z for Zero—close the book!" (*ABC*).

In simple verse that appeals to a young child, Gág devised a story
about a young rabbit. As the little bunny sleeps, an apple falls out of a
tree. It scares him into running. He meets a frog, lizard, and porcupine
family along the way; then he eats greens for lunch before dashing down
a bunny hole. Insects, vegetables, and fruit are interspersed with the letters, inspired by Gág's garden. The story propels the bunny from episode
to episode, in which it encounters a hail storm and a number of creatures.

With the text finalized, she embarked on the illustrations. She
sketched a rabbit for almost every page, except the first, which has an

apple. She wrote to a fan, "I went to a place in our village where there were hundreds of rabbits (the wild ones were too elusive for sketching) and there I made pages and pages of sketches" (Gág to Mary Griffen, 10 October 1936, CLRC). Despite the change in wording describing the frog from the tentative "a funny clown" to "he's fat and funny" in the final version, she retained the spotted clown suit in the illustration (manuscript for *ABC*, CLRC).

Meanwhile, the Coward-McCann editorial staff discussed the proposed titles, discarding "ABC Book" or "Wanda Gág's ABC" and settling on *The ABC Bunny*. In consultation with her publisher, Gág invited her sister Flavia to compose music to accompany the text, to appear on the endpapers, and urged Howard to render the lettering. Lacking a piano at All Creation, Flavia arranged to use a neighbor's instrument. Gág accompanied her occasionally to listen to the progress. In the middle of all this, Flavia went to New York City for a kidney stone operation.

That was not the only cause for distress for Gág. The production manager insisted that she draw the original twenty-nine illustrations on white paper, despite her plea that she draw on zinc plates. He calculated the appropriate dimensions, assuring her they could be reproduced in the same size. The first proofs pulled in March proved him wrong, however, as the rich tones and subtle grays were lost. Gág redrew nineteen of the illustrations, this time on zinc; but lithographs drawn on zinc plates with lithographic crayon is exacting work—the process tolerates no erasures or changes. Not only did Gág lose a month and a half repeating the work for the lithographs, but the late June and July heat caused the crayons to melt. "I am almost frantic with trying to get off the last entry of ABC," Gág wrote in her diary. "CMC [Coward-McCann] are getting panicky about it. I can't sleep well or eat well because of the strain of forcing myself to work more hours than I really feel equal to" (Diary, 17 July 1933). She finally completed the work, however, and the twenty-eight full-page drawings awaited the next stage in printing. Howard made the letters, which would be printed in red. It was ironic that *The ABC Bunny,* which celebrated nature, demanded that Gág work in her studio. She yearned to work outside, but could not because the project was so exacting. The process would not tolerate a mistake or even a bit of dirt.

George C. Miller, a fine printer, also contended with the heat. High temperatures ruined a week's work in the process of making transfers. Then Gág had to go to the printing plant to draw plates for the red and green colors for the cover. Finally, by mid-August, Miller considered his work "about ninety percent perfect" and mailed the press sheets to Gág for

her acceptance. At Gág's urging, the publisher agreed to buy expensive
high-quality paper for the first printing to ensure good images. In the
end, carefully supervised procedures resulted in a handsome book.
Gág dedicated the book to her sister Stella's son and her only nephew,
Gary Harm. The thirty-two page book sold for $2. *The ABC Bunny* was
another example of Gág's good sense of bookmaking. When opened, the
back and front covers together held asymmetrical balance. Just the right
number of green leaves with alphabet letters in red ink and appropriate
white spaces are set against the black background. The endpapers with
Flavia's "ABC Song" repeat the same color scheme and introduce the
hand-lettering used for the interior text.

In September 1933, Gág entered in her diary that the next day was
scheduled for "ABC's release, and mine, too, in a sense" (Diary, 17
September 1933). Dobbs wrote, "I think it's the best thing you've done
so far—even better than the Cats, and you know what sacrilege it is to
say anything like that" (Dobbs to Gág, 5 September 1933, CLRC).

Reviewer Eaton commented in the *New York Times Book Review* on the
"freshness of invention, and the drawings, the beauty, humor and originality characteristic of this artist's work."[18] Writing for the *Saturday
Review of Literature*, Alice Dalgliesh concluded, "Wanda Gág has a feeling
for the rightness of words that no other maker of picture books can
approach."[19]

Admirers, too, sent their congratulations. After seeing the proofs, Viking
Press editor May Massee wrote Gág a letter in which she called *The ABC
Bunny* "one of the loveliest children's books I have ever seen. It is just perfect and has the same sort of quiet that there always is around a little
bunny." She advised Gág to refrain from illustrating books by others, "even
when they are as wonderful as Grimm's," and signed her letter, "Sincerely
and most enthusiastically, May Massee" (Massee to Gág, 22 August 1933,
CLRC). Gág's publisher Thomas Coward wrote a note by hand, telling her
the book was a masterpiece. "If we can't sell it either we are no good or the
public is blind. . . . It's a real excitement to publish anything as distinguished and as gay. . . . There is so much that is shoddy in this [publishing
business], as in every other game, that such a book is like brook water after
being lost in a desert" (Coward to Gág, 5 September 1933, CLRC). He
later asked her to come to the office to autograph about twenty-five books
for distribution to influential people. Gág, too, thought the book looked
"pretty good. When I had finished the job I was so sick of it I wondered if
anyone would ever be interested in buying it. . . . That does not mean I can
count on large sales as the times are too uncertain for that" (Diary, 1935).

Creating an alphabet book is risky because it is inevitably compared with the others published during the same season and with those held up as historical models. Any story is easier to recall than individual images. Gág's was not the only alphabet book published in 1933. Even her acquaintance Rene d'Harnoncourt illustrated one—*Beast, Bird, and Fish: An Animal Alphabet*[20]—which incorporated music as did Gág's. Although that book lacked a plot, Gág considered it more sophisticated than her own. But Gág's *ABC Bunny* fares well, both in a first reading and in memory. The artist was skilled in planning and making lithographs, a medium with which she'd worked for years. The large format design and clear images make it possible for a youngster to "read" the pictures even without the text.

Following publication, Gág promoted *The ABC Bunny*. She autographed copies in the toy department of Saks Fifth Avenue, spoke at the Little Red School House in New York City, and traveled in November to Buffalo and Cleveland. On her return from the Children's Book Week trip, she drafted a letter to Thomas Coward noting that the book was "enthusiastically received" and that despite printing limitations, it "looks just as I wanted and expected it to look" (Gág to Coward, 21 November 1933, CLRC). Because of expected low sales during the Depression, the publisher withheld its complete binding order, but by December sales merited binding the entire printing.

To entice the Newbery Award committee members of the American Library Association, the publisher sent copies to them and Dobbs monitored their individual reactions. At least four responded to the publisher. Three members used the word "charming," and a fourth added, "It is somewhat of an achievement to make a new ABC book." Nonetheless, the 1934 Newbery Award for books published the previous year went to Cornelia Meig's *Invincible Louisa,* a biography about Louisa May Alcott.[21] Ironically, Alcott was an author whom Gág admired for her tenacity in working toward a career as a writer despite poverty and for her literary achievements. Along with seven other books, Gág's *The ABC Bunny* achieved Newbery Honor Book status.

The year 1933 proved arduous as the U.S. economy suffered and President Franklin Delano Roosevelt declared a bank holiday to prevent people from withdrawing their money. Gág's two cats, Snoopy and Nuppins, died the same year. Although she discussed the possibility of a Brothers Grimm edition and a "Story of My Childhood" with Coward-McCann, Gág was exhausted and insisted on a break from children's books the following year. She vowed that her next projects would be dedicated to drawing. "They won't be able to rope me into a book next year and I've told them so. In fact, outside from doing Grimm's fairy tales within the next two or three years, I doubt whether I'll do another juvenile for years to come. It's what I live on, I know, and I couldn't have lived on my drawings and prints the last three years, but even so, the time has come for the drawings and prints whether there's a market for them or not. I've just got to draw the things around me for a while—so much has been piling up in my mind" (Gág to Newton, 19 August 1933, CLRC). Indeed, Gág skipped a year before her next book was published. During the winter, she pasted clippings into her "Blaa Book" and worked on a self-portrait and other drawings. She spent some time in the fall of 1934 working on a series of essays based on her childhood memories, which she called "Reminiscences."

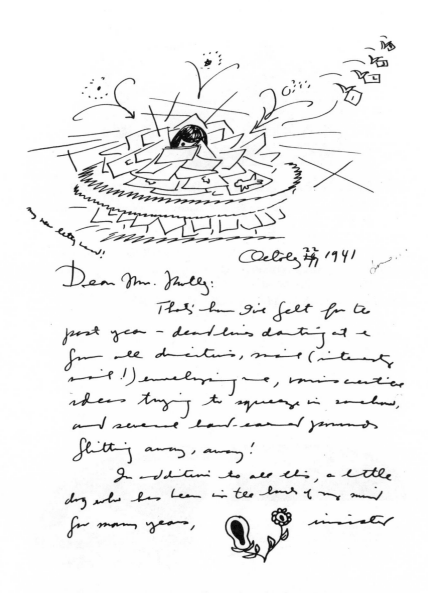

DRAFT IN INK BY WANDA GÁG OF A LETTER. SHE OCCASIONALLY
ADDED A DRAWING TO CORRESPONDENCE TO ADULTS AND
FREQUENTLY TO CHILDREN.

Reprinted by permission of the CLRC and of Gary Harm.

WANDA GÁG: *35 years of picture-making*

A RETROSPECTIVE SHOW AT *The Weyhe Gallery* 794 LEXINGTON AVENUE

OCTOBER 12 TO OCTOBER 31 · 1940

INVITATION BY WANDA GÁG, INCLUDING HER CURRENT TRANSLATION
PROJECT AND THE INEVITABLE CAT, FOR A RETROSPECTIVE EXHIBIT AT
THE WEYHE GALLERY IN NEW YORK CITY, 12–31 OCTOBER 1940.
In the CLRC. Reprinted by permission of the CLRC and of Gary Harm.

And so he went back over the sunny hills and
down through the cool valleys, to show all his
pretty kittens to the very old woman.
   It was very funny to see those hundreds and
thousands and millions and billions and trillions
of cats following him.

INK ILLUSTRATION BY WANDA GÁG SHOWING HER USE OF THE
DOUBLE-PAGE SPREAD FOR *MILLIONS OF CATS*.
*In the CLRC. Reprinted by permission of the CLRC, Gary Harm, and the Putnam & Grosset
Group. Millions of Cats copyright 1928 by Coward-McCann, Inc., copyright renewed.*

INK STUDY BY WANDA GÁG OF THE TWO MICE FACING A MIRROR FOR
SNIPPY AND SNAPPY.

*In the CLRC, Reprinted by permission of the CLRC, Gary Harm, and the Putnam & Grosset
Group.* Snippy and Snappy *copyright 1931 by Coward-McCann, Inc., copyright renewed.*

INK STUDY COMPLETED SEVEN YEARS BEFORE PUBLICATION OF
THE FUNNY THING.
In the CLRC. Reprinted by permission of the CLRC, Gary Harm, and the Putnam & Grosset
Group. The Funny Thing *copyright 1929 by Coward-McCann, Inc., copyright renewed.*

LITHOGRAPH STUDY BY WANDA GÁG WITH A FROG WITH "CLOWN
SPOTS" FROM THE WORKING TEXT FOR *THE ABC BUNNY*.
*In the CLRC. Reprinted by permission of the CLRC, Gary Harm, and the Putnam & Grosset
Group.* The ABC Bunny *copyright 1933 by Coward-McCann, Inc., copyright renewed.*

TWO INK STUDIES BY WANDA GÁG OF THE TRADITIONAL STORYTELLER
RETELLING A STORY AND FRITZL DOING DOMESTIC WORK FOR *GONE IS
GONE, OR THE STORY OF A MAN WHO WANTED TO DO HOUSEWORK.*
*In the CLRC. Reprinted by permission of the CLRC, Gary Harm, and the Putnam & Grosset
Group.* Gone Is Gone, or The Story of a Man Who Wanted to Do Housework *copyright
1935 by Coward-McCann, Inc., copyright renewed.*

THREE INK STUDIES BY WANDA GÁG OF FRITZL LEADING THE COW
AND OF THE ROPE TIED BETWEEN THE COW ON THE ROOF AND FRITZL
IN THE KITCHEN, WHICH CAUSES NEAR-DISASTER IN *GONE IS GONE OR,
THE STORY OF A MAN WHO WANTED TO DO HOUSEWORK.*

*In the CLRC. Reprinted by permission of the CLRC, Gary Harm, and the Putnam & Grosset
Group.* Gone Is Gone, or The Story of a Man Who Wanted to Do Housework *copyright
1935 by Coward-McCann, Inc., copyright renewed.*

INK STUDY BY WANDA GÁG FOR THE BOOK JACKET OF *THREE GAY
TALES FROM GRIMM*.

*In the CLRC. Reprinted by permission of the CLRC, Gary Harm, and the Putnam & Grosset
Group.* Three Gay Tales from Grimm *copyright 1943 by Coward-McCann, Inc., copyright
renewed.*

TWO INK STUDIES BY WANDA GÁG OF THE PRINCE SIMPLE SEPP IN "THE
THREE FEATHERS," ONE OF THE THREE STORIES IN *THREE GAY TALES
FROM GRIMM*, P. 29.

*In the CLRC. Reprinted by permission of the CLRC, Gary Harm, and the Putnam & Grosset
Group.* Three Gay Tales from Grimm *copyright 1943 by Coward-McCann, Inc., copyright
renewed.*

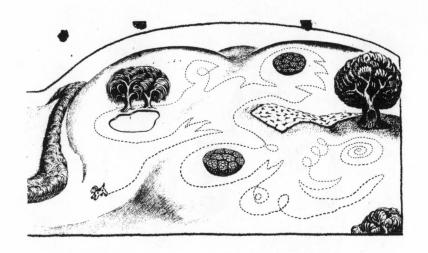

INK STUDY BY WANDA GÁG SHOWING THE DOG'S PATH WHEN HE
BECOMES VISIBLE AND ILLUSTRATING HER USE OF "FACETS AND
MERIDIANS" FOR *NOTHING AT ALL.*
In the CLRC. Reprinted by permission of the CLRC, Gary Harm, and the Putnam & Grosset
Group. Nothing at All *copyright 1941 by Coward-McCann, Inc., copyright renewed.*

INK STUDY BY WANDA GÁG, WITH REPETITION OF THE WING-LIKE
DESIGN, FOR "THE TAILOR WHO WENT TO HEAVEN," IN *MORE TALES
FROM GRIMM*, P. 120.
In the CLRC. Reprinted by permission of the CLRC, Gary Harm, and the Putnam & Grosset
Group. More Tales from Grimm *copyright 1947 by Coward-McCann, Inc., copyright renewed.*

INK STUDY BY WANDA GÁG FOR "THE WOLF AND THE SEVEN LITTLE
KIDS," IN *MORE TALES FROM GRIMM*, P. 241.

*In the CLRC. Reprinted by permission of the CLRC, Gary Harm, and the Putnam & Grosset
Group.* More Tales from Grimm *copyright 1947 by Coward-McCann, Inc., copyright renewed.*

INK STUDY BY WANDA GÁG, INCLUDING A CAT FOLLOWING THE
BOY, FOR "THE SORCERER'S APPRENTICE," IN *MORE TALES FROM GRIMM*,
P. 205.

*In the CLRC. Reprinted by permission of the CLRC, Gary Harm, and the Putnam & Grosset
Group.* More Tales from Grimm *copyright 1947 by Coward-McCann, Inc., copyright renewed.*

INK STUDY BY WANDA GÁG, INCLUDING A CAT ON THE HEARTH, FOR
"THE SORCERER'S APPRENTICE," IN *MORE TALES FROM GRIMM,* P. 201.
*In the CLRC. Reprinted by permission of the CLRC, Gary Harm, and the Putnam & Grosset
Group.* More Tales from Grimm *copyright 1947 by Coward-McCann, Inc., copyright renewed.*

Chapter Four
Brothers Grimm Translated

German was an important language for American artists during the 1920s because many art theory and art history books appeared in German. During the decade, Gág read German books to refresh her childhood memory of the language. She wrote to her friend Harold Larrabee in 1923, "So many good art books are in German that I've decided to regain what I once knew of the language and add more to it besides" (Gág to Larrabee, 31 July 1923, CLRC). A year later, Gág reiterated her progress: "I have been studying German assiduously in the form of translating . . . for linguistic and artistic reasons" (Gág to Larrabee, 21 October 1924, CLRC). In 1927 Gág sought Larrabee's advice about which substantial German-English dictionary to buy. To practice the language, Gág read the Brothers Grimm fairy tales in German and then began to translate selected stories. Moreover, she envisioned illustrating fifty or sixty of the two hundred known Brothers Grimm fairy tales for a three-volume set of books.

More than a century earlier, the brothers Jakob and Wilhelm Grimm, both linguists, had transcribed the fairy tales from the oral tradition. A publisher in Berlin printed them in two collections, one in 1812 and the second in 1815. English translations appeared in 1823 and 1826, respectively. Because the United States did not participate in the International Copyright Agreement until 1891, many American trade publishers reproduced European and British books liberally without paying royalties to the authors, translators, or illustrators across the Atlantic Ocean. American publishers made these fairy tales by the Brothers Grimm widely available as collected or as individual tales in both German and English. Publishers D. C. Heath in Boston, Henry Holt in New York, and the American Book Company in Cincinnati produced German-language editions from 1885 to 1903. Meanwhile, publishers such as T. Y. Crowell brought the Lucy Crane translations and J. B. Lippincott brought the Mrs. Edgar Lucas translations to the United States. Ticknor and Fields produced *Grimm's Goblins* in 1867, using a selection from the previously published collection *Household Stories of the Brothers Grimm,* which was illustrated by George Cruikshank. Textbook publishers produced individual fairy tales or incorporated them in readers. For example, in 1903, University Publishing Company in New York adapted a selection of stories for pupils at the third-grade reading level, titled *Grimm's Best Stories.*

English-language translations of Jakob and Wilhelm Grimm's *Kinder-und Hausmärchen* abounded before the 1930s in both England and the United States. Translators and illustrators in England interpreted Grimm for English-reading audiences. American publishers then reprinted the same works for several decades. This procedure was cheaper than paying for a new American translator and illustrator. Therefore, the American public read editions translated by Crane or Lucas and illustrated by Englishmen George Cruikshank, Walter Crane, Richard Doyle, Leslie Brooke, or others. These British editions then appeared in American libraries. As early as 1882, a Hartford, Connecticut librarian, Caroline Hewins, compiled a list of selected books for American children to read. Intended for national distribution, the publication included the Brothers Grimm fairy tales.[1] Even after the passing of the international copyright regulation in 1891, the American publishers continued to reproduce the English editions. But the English books could no longer be pirated. After 1891 the American publisher by law had to recognize the copyright from another country. Arthur Rackham, a distinguished English artist, illustrated the Brothers Grimm for two decades beginning in 1900. E. P. Dutton could then publish in 1920 the American edition of Constable's *Hansel and Grethel and Other Tales,* illustrated by Rackham, but had to make financial arrangements.

By the twentieth century, Americans, too, were translating and illustrating the Brothers Grimm fairy tales. At least three published within a fourteen year span had the same title, *Grimm's Fairy Tales.* Githa Sowerby retold and Millicent Sowerby illustrated for the publisher F. A. Stokes in 1910.[2] Cupples and Leon published Margaret Hunt's translation illustrated by John B. Gruelle only four years later.[3] Ernest Beeson translated and George Soper illustrated an edition for George H. Doran in 1924.[4] English immigrant Louis John Rhead and Danish immigrant Kay Nielsen also illustrated Grimm. By the 1920s, each of the major American trade publishing companies had promoted its own version of the Brothers Grimm fairy tales. It was to Gág's advantage that Coward-McCann was a new company in 1928. This opened the door for her to provide the publisher with a new edition of the Brothers Grimm.

Librarians themselves championed fairy tales, and that was also to Gág's advantage. For four centuries, educators had debated the potential benefit or harm of fairy tales to children. Educators Jean-Jacques Rosseau,

Sarah Trimmer, and Lucy Sprague Mitchell from the eighteenth, nineteenth, and twentieth century, respectively demanded more realistic literature for children and decried fairy tales and fables. On the other hand, the seventeenth-century English philosopher John Locke recommended *Aesop* and *Reynard the Fox*. His point of view was upheld by authors Charles Lamb and Charles Dickens and updated by the twentieth-century psychiatrist Bruno Bettelheim.

With the assistance of Anne Carroll Moore, children's specialist at the New York Public Library, Gág found two books of great importance to her next project. One was a copy of the Brothers Grimm fairy tales in English translation with an introduction by John Ruskin[5]; the other was Marie L. Shedlock's *The Art of the Storyteller*.[6] Inspired by the visits to America by this English expert at the turn of the century, the library had initiated story hours and encouraged storytelling. Shedlock herself lectured on storytelling in major cities in the East and Midwest. In 1934, the *Horn Book* devoted a special issue to the subject of storytelling in honor of Shedlock's eightieth birthday. Moore's lead article was entitled, "Our Fairy Godmother, Marie L. Shedlock." Mary Gould Davis, the New York Public Library staff storyteller who often told stories by Gág, contributed an essay, "The Story-Teller's Art," to the *Horn Book* in 1934.[7] Thus, Shedlock's lectures and the prominent magazine's focus on storytelling had prepared children's librarians across the nation for Gág's editions of the Brothers Grimm.

When Gág read Grimm as an adult, as part of her renewed interest in the German language, she "was surprised at the wealth of information which these stories yielded."[8] They seemed rich with historical insight into the old German way of life, with details about clothing, food, and furniture. While reading these fairy tales, Gág recalled her father's folios in their New Ulm home. She remembered the pictures of German peasants and Swiss mountains. Significantly, Gág was one of only a few Americans who could both translate and illustrate an edition of the Brothers Grimm. She had from childhood spoken German in her hometown of New Ulm and with her relatives; and she continued to use the language while attending art schools in the Twin Cities because friends Edgar Hermann and Adolf Dehn both spoke German. Humphreys, her brother-in-law Robert Janssen, and Zigrosser also knew German.

Beginning in 1932, Gág translated Grimm's fairy tales over a four-year period. During that year the editor of the *New York Herald Tribune*'s first Children's Book Week Section asked her to submit a drawing for the holiday issue. It was to accompany an article by May Lamberton Becker entitled "Parents: Let No Child Go Hungry for Books." Prompted by her renewed interest in German fairy tales, Gág drew an illustration of Hansel and Gretel in front of the witch's candy house. The caption concluded, "In my illustration I have tried to show what 'Märchen' [fairy tales] means to me—a magic word to which I hope I'll never cease to react."[9]

This single drawing made an enormous impact. Readers assumed erroneously that the drawing was an advertisement for an already published Wanda Gág book, and Coward-McCann received orders for the as yet nonexistent publication. The trend-setting Moore asked to borrow the drawing for her New York Public Library children's room display. May Massee, the prestigious Viking Press editor, invited Gág to lunch, adding the caveat that if she had already planned a Grimm publication with another publisher, she would not continue to pursue her. "I do wish you'd let me see you some time soon," she wrote, adding that Gág and Miska Petersham were the two people who had "really done something for children in this country" (Massee to Gág, 4 January 1933, CLRC). Gág remained loyal to Coward-McCann.

The important triangle of author-illustrator, publisher, and public was poised for a Brothers Grimm book illustrated by Gág. She characteristically mobilized her friends and acquaintances. Zigrosser located a copy of Grimm in the original German for her to keep at home so she did not have to rely on library copies. Then Moore introduced her to the concept of variant editions and advised her how she might translate more freely. Moore suggested further that Gág choose tales appropriate to children and gave her hints about handling the violence in the stories. Moreover, Moore encouraged her to illustrate the tales in a manner similar to the newspaper drawing of "Hansel and Gretel." Anne T. Eaton, a staff member at the Lincoln School, Columbia University's Teachers College, in addition to being a reviewer, guided her to other translators of Grimm for models, such as collections by Mrs. Edward V. Lucas and Lucy Crane.

Winter blizzards in 1932 and 1933 left Gág snowbound at All Creation; even the mailman and coalman could not get there. Because the family had to substitute wood for coal in the furnace, the house was too cold for drawing. Gág stayed in bed under quilts (her favorite setting for writing) and wrote and rewrote a dozen translations of Grimm. Meanwhile, she neglected her diary—not because she was busy but because she simply didn't feel like writing in it (Diary, 12 May 1935). Instead she concentrated on what would become *Gone Is Gone* and *Tales from Grimm.*

Gone Is Gone

One story Wanda Gág remembered from her childhood, "The Man Who Wanted to Do Housework," proved elusive. She couldn't remember having seen it recently. Moreover, she could not recall which of her relatives had told the story; her parents, grandparents, Aunts Mary and Lena, and her Uncle Frank had all been storytellers. Searching again, she could not locate it among the two hundred Grimm tales she had read, and it did not occur to her to pursue Norwegian fairy tales. Perhaps she had read "The Husband Who Was to Mind the House" in Gudrun Thorne-Thomsen's *East o' the Sun and West o' the Moon*, published in 1912 when she was nineteen. But that version described a pig rather than a dog entering the kitchen. She only recalled the story about a man who considered his field work difficult and his wife's domestic chores easy. He suggested that they change work roles. The wife then went into the fields for the day, with a scythe over her shoulder, and returned feeling self-satisfied. The man proved inept at handling domestic tasks.

This story appealed to Gág's sense of humor and feminist leanings. "As a child I thought it irresistibly funny, especially when the man got whisked up into the chimney and the cow on her rope hung over the edge of the roof . . . my mental picture of the cow grazing on the grassy roof was still very vivid in my memory" (Diary, 1935). The story demonstrates what a variety of skills a housekeeper needs. Gág herself did not enjoy domestic work, but she detested disorganization more. Her parents had set a high standard in housekeeping, which she had continued. As a teenager she tasted the bitterness of staying home from high school half-days to assist with the housework. She now used income from her book royalties to pay her youngest sister, Flavia, to handle the household chores and to type her manuscripts and correspondence.

Gág decided this unidentified story would be her next book project. "Suddenly it occurred to me that I might make a little book of this story by itself. . . . I told them [Coward-McCann] it would have to be a dollar book" (Diary, 22 or 26 February 1935). The publisher agreed, as the Depression prevented sales of high-priced books. Gág embellished the story she remembered with her own style and flair for words. The Danish fairy-tale author Hans Christian Andersen was a model, for he superimposed a literary style on the stories he had heard or read. For the dust jacket copy, Gág wrote, "I decided to make a little book of the story, consulting no other sources except one—my own memory of how the tale was told to me when I was a little girl."

Giving the book the tentative title "Turn & Turn About," she worked on the text but temporarily abandoned the project when it didn't crystalize. For a while, she wrote in the present tense, remembering how some storytellers handle fairy tales—"Now Fritzl runs to the top of the stairs, and what does he see?"—but that seemed too unwieldy. Then she tried the past tense, which seemed more appropriate. She had also experimented with the name of the protagonist, who might be "Fritzerli" or "Frenzl," and she settled on "Fritzl." The wife, child, and dog remained "Liesi" (close to her own mother's nickname, Lissi), "Kinndli," and "Spitz," respectively. Gág perfected parallel participles to describe the butter churn, "tipping, falling, spilling." Additional images included the lyrical, such as "angel's eyes blinking in the grass." She avoided the English expressions, "Presto" and "Alackaday," and inserted more Germanic phrases, such as "Na, Na," "Hulla! Hey, hi, ho, hulla!" and "Ritsch, rotsch" instead. Recalling her prior year's vegetable garden, she listed potatoes, onions, carrots, cabbages, beets, beans, turnips, parsley, and celery in the roster of plantings. Near the end of the text, the husband begged to return to the fields when his wife suggested that housework would become easier in time.

The book opens with a personal testimony of the passing on of a story in the oral tradition from generation to generation. Gág tells the story with vigor: "Well, Liesi lost no time the next morning. There she was at peep of day, striding across the fields with a jug of water in her hand and the scythe over her shoulder" (*Gone*). Action is picture-clear: "he turned back, puffing and panting, and mopping his face with his big red handkerchief (*Gone*)." Gág prepares the child reader for unfamiliar circumstances. For example, knowing that the cow will graze on the roof, she writes: "Fritzl's house was not covered with shingles or tin or tile—it was covered with . . . a fine crop of grass" (*Gone*). Rearranging the words lends a traditional storytelling tenor to the text. "Noontime it was, no dinner made" and "that work of yours, tis none too easy" (*Gone*). But the story's real success depends partly on the situational comedy of the war between the sexes and partly on Gág's vibrant language in her retelling.

In addition to refining the text, Gág wanted to establish a humorous tone. She recalled that the story had been irresistibly funny, for "the chuckle, the sly dry humor, the simple form, the salty peasant style, all these came back to me, and suddenly it seemed to me that was the way the story which was not in Grimm should be written" (Diary, 1935).

Gág discussed the possibility of the publication with Thomas Coward and fellow staff members. Editor Rose Dobbs discovered that a similar fairy tale was in a collection published the previous decade, but Veronica Hutchinson's version, "The Husband Who Was Left to Mind the House," included in *Candle-Light Stories,* lacked a satisfying ending.[10] The last episode brought no resolution, concluding with "down came her husband out of the chimney; and so when his goody came inside the kitchen, there she found him standing on his head in the porridge pot" (Hutchinson, 89).

In Gág's version, the wife returned home from the field to find the cow dangling from the roof, the animals eating in the garden, the child covered with churned butter, the dog satiated with sausages, cider spilled on the floor, and vegetable peelings strewn all over the kitchen. To her final astonishment, her husband was in the soup kettle over the fire. Gág explained that when the cow's rope was cut, Fritzl fell down the chimney into the kettle of soup. She hastened to add that Liesi rescued him. The text continued with a gentle conversation between the two in which Fritzl said that he will no longer consider Liesi's work less difficult than his. Moreover, Liesi suggested, "if that's how it is, we surely can live in peace and happiness for ever and ever," and the story concluded, "And that they did" (*Gone*).

After completing the text to her satisfaction, Gág made a rough dummy layout in fall 1934 and began illustrating in December. By Christmastime of that year, she commented that she was dissatisfied with the drawings. Gág considered abandoning the project, but she ultimately had faith in the story. She analyzed the situation and decided that she was limiting herself by stylizing the costumes. Then she went upstairs to her room and "day after day and doggedly gave birth to various Fritzls, Liesis, and Kindlis. This procedure if kept up long enough (and provided of course one has a good kernel to work with) usually gets results. By stumbling around in all directions we finally stumbled upon the right solution, in case we can't get it any other way. Gradually my rough sketches began to build up into a certain rightness (that is, it seemed so to me) and as I unfolded episode after episode, the characters became real people to me" (Diary, 1935). Fritzl's grumpiness, his wife's patience, and the child's plainness developed from her pencil, and for them "a deep respect & fondness grew up within me" (Diary, 1935).

To develop the characters, Gág called upon impressions of the German-Austrian-Bohemian peasant immigrant group she remembered from New Ulm. "On Sundays the men got dressed up in fancy knee breeches with colorful embroidery on their suspenders. And the women, in calico aprons and kerchiefs on their heads, ran barefooted while they herded their geese" (Diary, 1935). Not only did Gág attend to the costumes, but she also positioned the characters carefully on each page. The toddler's pose of sleeping with thumb in mouth, and the antics of the child eating a flower, chewing on a pretzel, and climbing up on the butter churn indicate keen observation of early childhood behavior. Careful planning resulted in pictures that match perfectly with the text. The picture of Fritzl watching the liquid pour from the barrel reflects the previous story line of his anticipating an apple cider drink with sausage. Also, numerous details in the illustrations serve to corroborate the text. For example, as Liesi pulls two arms and two legs from the soup kettle, "there, dripping and spluttering, with a cabbage-leaf in his hair, celery in his pocket, and a sprig of parsley over one ear, was her Fritzl" (Gone).

Gág made a mock-up of the text and illustrations, which she took to Coward-McCann. She proposed a square book about half the width of her first three oblong picture books. Then she embarked on final pen and ink illustrations. Finally, Gone Is Gone was ready for the engraver and then for the printer in July. Correcting the proofs, approving the paper, and "checking this and that have dragged out. . . . But of course this didn't take a lot of time, only frequent attention" (Gág to Zigrosser, 13 July 1935). She dedicated the book "To My Peasant Ancestors."

The sixty-four page book, Gone Is Gone: The Story of a Man Who Wanted to Do Housework, was ready for fall publication. Its diminutive size was deceptive, for it was a gem of prose and illustration. The book received complimentary reviews. Laura Benet, in New York Herald Tribune Books, commented that the book was reminiscent of Bohemian storytelling, "supplied with plenty of fat little pictures in the same spirit; it makes one of the smallest and funniest story books of the season."[11] Eaton's recommendation that it would be appropriate for children aged five to nine limits the audience, for adults enjoy the story, too. She was right, however, that it is suitable "for reading aloud and will also appeal to those beginning to read for themselves." She forecast that it "makes us eager for the illustrated edition of Grimm which, it is rumored, Miss Gág is preparing."[12] Marjorie F. Potter reiterated the appeal of Gone Is Gone to storytellers in Library Journal. She noted its "added flavor and a heightened sense of drama and humor."[13] Moore ordered eighty-four copies for the New York Public Library and its branches and asked to borrow the colorful frontispiece for display.

As the Newbery Award garnered even more prestige through the years, editors yearned for this recognition for their authors. Gág's editor wrote to her, "If only the . . . librarians would have the sense to see that the Newbery medal really belongs to you this year. We'll try to see if anything can be done" (Dobbs to Gág, 18 September 1935, CLRC). Receiving the Newbery Award would assure book sales for the winner, but *Gone Is Gone* did not even attain honor status. The Newbery Award in 1936 for books published the previous year went to another Minnesotan, Carol Ryrie Brink. Her historic fiction book, *Caddie Woodlawn*, described in part her grandmother's childhood in the adjacent state of Wisconsin.[14] Coincidentally, the setting for Phil Stong's *Honk the Moose*, one of the four Honor Books, was a northern Minnesota mining town.

To attract more sales for the British edition, Faber and Faber bound the book in pink buckram for its printing in 1936. Even selling foreign rights such as these did not solve financial problems. Trouble descended on Coward-McCann because of lack of sales during the Depression, affecting Gág's finances.

Therefore, when a *Smart Magazine* staff member suggested that Gág sell stories to magazines, she followed the advice. By 1935 she finished a short original story, "The Cry-Away Bird," to submit to an adult journal, the *Delineator*.[15] An engraver transferred to copper only four of the five ink illustrations drawn to accompany the text, because the story with illustrations was printed on a single page. In this new story, the problem-solver is the same old man of the mountains as in *The Funny Thing*, published six years earlier. Now Bobo coaches a tearful bird. Under his tutelage, the crane-like bird—which cried incessantly over such things as "Christmas comes only once a year," "ink makes black spots," and "purple is never yellow"—begins to laugh. This story revealed a private aspect of Gág's personality—overcoming grief stalwartly. Outwardly strong in her youth when making decisions with and for her siblings, Gág succumbed to crying in private and occasionally streaked her adolescent diaries with tears. At the end of the story, the bird's name changes to "Smile-Away." Gág's financial situation also called for smiles; the *Delineator* paid her $100.

Gág then offered the *Gone Is Gone* story to *Child Life* magazine. The company published the text in the December 1935 issue with a variant title, "A Man Who Wanted to Do Housework: An Old Tale Retold and Illustrated by Wanda Gág."[16] Gág arranged the drawings in a different sequence and added sausage-shaped borders enhanced by green and red ink.

Fortunately for Gág, payments for the magazine stories and the fall book financed the building of a guest house at All Creation. Her studio could now be used exclusively for work, rather than doubling as sleeping

space for company. Gág continued her daily routine of walking up the
hill to her studio. In rainy weather she wore high rubber boots, in cold
weather her father's old gray cape. Hidden under the coat was a brown
basket with eyeglasses, green eyeshades for too-sunny days, and a ther-
mos of coffee (Flavia Gag Papers).

In 1935, Gág continued to resist offers from book publishers other
than Coward-McCann. The general manager of Albert Whitman had
asked her to illustrate a fairy-tale book (F. D. Knapp to Gág, 2 October
1935, CLRC), but she refused. Consequently, Laura May Bannon got the
job for James Cloyd Bowman and Margery Bianco's *Tales from a Finnish
Tupa* instead. Bannon also illustrated Bowman's *Pecos Bill*, another popular book on Whitman's list.

Tales from Grimm

After four years of working on the Grimm translations, Gág planned to
illustrate them early in 1936. Her sister Nelda's illness necessitated a
postponement of these plans. When Nelda's streptococcus infection
became life threatening, Gág's medical doctor friends used an experimental drug. By coincidence, the drug had arrived in New York City
just that morning. Nelda was consequently the first recipient in the
country of prontisil, a sulfa wonder drug (Scott, 178–79). When Nelda
recovered it was summer, the time Gág usually liked to paint. Instead, as
she wrote in her diary, she worked on the Brothers Grimm book. "I saw
people taking sunbaths, playing games. . . . I had to sit at my table and
draw and draw. My eyes were giving me a lot of trouble, but I didn't
seem to have enough time to go to town and get glasses" (Diary, 1936).

Gág envisioned three volumes for the Grimm collection, with a total of
sixty stories. As she progressed on the project, she chose and translated
tales and sought advice from others. "I plan to select some of the most
amusing and least gory stories, make my own translations, and illustrate
them," she wrote to a friend (Gág to Ellis Seymour, 13 August 1934,
CLRC). Gág's early preferences were "Snow White," "Three Feathers," and
"Golden Key," but none of these made it into the first volume.

The stories Gág chose to illustrate reflected her personality in many
ways. Her appreciation of droll humor prompted her to choose "Clever
Elsie," which is predicated on nonsense. In addition, Gág's dislike of
arrogance finds a satisfactory ending in "The Fisherman and His Wife."
The story points a finger at haughtiness and greed. Finding herself the
king, the emperor, and finally the pope, the greedy woman is relegated

to the vinegar jug when she has the audacity to expect to "be like God" (*Tales,* 168). The moral in "Lazy Heinz" agreed with Gág's work ethic. Heinz and his wife, Fat Katrina, talk about the child they will have who will tend the geese they will buy. But they sleep until noon, and will inevitably fail in every endeavor they attempt.

The "Cinderella" tale suited Gág especially, for the heroine resists the temptation to collapse under hardship. Both Cinderella and Gág offset their respective burdens with hard work. When the stepmother and her two haughty daughters leave for the ball, Gág's "Cinderella did not mope and cry as you might suppose. Instead, she suddenly became very busy" (*Tales,* 108). The Grimm Brothers' "Cinderella," unlike Frenchman Charles Perrault's version, has a different concept of the fairy godmother. In fact, Gág's editor suggested "something in the preface to dispel the qualms of fairy godmother fans" (Dobbs to Gág, 16 June 1936, CLRC). The more familiar French version by Perrault from 1797 highlighted the fairy godmother as an important character; the Grimm version lacks such a character. In her introduction, Gág explains that the Cinderella story "exists in one form or another in the folklore of many countries. . . . The familiar pumpkin-coach version is not included even in the alternative variants. Therefore it cannot be called a Grimm 'Märchen' and I did not feel justified in using it" (*Tales,* xii).

Cats figure prominently in both the text and illustrations in these tales. As in *Millions of Cats,* Gág depicts the distinctive features of cats in "Cat and Mouse Keep House." The protagonist, a "tawny yellow cat with sea-green eyes" (*Tales,* 27), is invited to the christenings of a kitten, "white with brown spots" (*Tales,* 29), "silvery grey with a white ring around its neck" (*Tales,* 31), and "pure black except for its paws and whiskers, which are white as the driven snow" (*Tales,* 32). Near the end, the cat follows its natural instincts and pounces on its prey, Grey-mouse, with whom he'd kept house. Gág translates the last sentence as, "Oh dear, that's the way things go in this world!" (*Tales,* 35). Another cat appears as one of the four animals in "The Musicians of Bremen." Here the old cat, which a robber mistook for "smouldering embers . . . sprang at him, spitting and scratching" (*Tales,* 95). Another reference to a cat in "Rapunzel," however, did not inspire a picture. Gág did add a black cat on the stoop of the house (*Tales,* 13), in the bedroom (*Tales,* 16), and behind the witch (*Tales,* 18) in "Hansel and Gretel," despite the lack of reference to a cat in the text.

While working on the translation of the Grimm fairy tales, Gág recognized many of the dialects used by the people of New Ulm, where her own family members had spoken a mixture of Bohemian and Bavarian dialects. Gág's German-born brother-in-law Robert Janssen assisted her with some of the less familiar dialects. Gág translated the text "freely" while writing the drafts by hand. As she completed each tale, Flavia typed it. Tellingly, Flavia Gag later inscribed a copy of *Tales from Grimm*, "During most of my lifetime I was caretaker, chief cook and bottle washer, and official typist for all of Wanda's books" (Flavia Gag to the author, May 1977, CLRC). Gág also consulted her companion Humphreys, who jotted suggestions about proposed word changes in red pencil at the bottom of some pages. Gág's aim was "to write readable, live, smooth-flowing prose. Most of the translations seem so stilted and unimaginative to me" (Gág to Alice Hancock, 4 February 1937, CLRC). For example, Gág sought a better word than "little" for the German *hanchen* and *hutchen*, but finally reverted to "little." While some of the fairy tales were too graphic for Gág to consider translating, they were helpful in developing her writing style.

Although "Hansel and Gretel" became the opening story in her sixteen-tale compilation, Gág used her color illustration of Rapunzel letting down her hair for the cover and the frontispiece. "Hansel and Gretel" instead had an interior illustration of the two children looking at the witch's house. It was almost an exact copy of the drawing she had made four years earlier for the *New York Herald Tribune* in 1932, for which she received warm, generous response. The drawing in the book lacks the chicken on the stoop, the duck in the bushes, and the crumbs dropped by Hansel. Additional door decorations are a gingerbread man, a pretzel, and hearts (*Tales,* 13). Recalling books from her own childhood, she intended to make her Grimm "Profusely Illustrated."

Near the end of the project, after Gág finished the text and illustrations, she dedicated the book "To Four Readers." Identified only by the letters "E," "C," "D," and "B," each letter was surrounded by a heart. The dedicatees may have been children, such as Eric Larrabee, or adults, such as Earle Humphreys and Carl Zigrosser.

Gág's 238-page *Tales from Grimm* sold for $1.50 and was highly successful when published in fall 1936. Macy's department store ordered 1,000 copies and the New York Public Library included the book in its *Children's Books Suggested as Holiday Gifts.*[17] It held up favorably even when compared with the 1937 Fritz Kredel edition, which was three times as large and translated by a German-born immigrant. Two of the individuals who had advised Gág earlier now judged the book: Moore reviewed it positively in the *Atlantic Monthly* and *Horn Book,* and Eaton praised it in the *New York Times Book Review.* "In her translations and in her drawings," Eaton writes, "Miss Gág has caught the essence of the fairy tale, its drama, its wonder, its joy, and with a fine freshness and zest she is bringing these qualities to boys and girls."[18] May Becker, the columnist for whom Gág drew the original Hansel and Gretel illustration, critiqued the book for the *New York Herald Tribune* book section. She addressed the need for a good translation of Grimm and commented on how Gág had fulfilled that need. In appraising the translation, she wrote that the rendition offers "the sense of spoken language; reading is like listening to a storyteller."[19]

The impact of the book is evident from Englishman Marcus Crouch's comment, almost three decades later, that "What makes Wanda Gág the most successful of all interpreters of Grimm is her fundamental lack of sophistication."[20] He admires her ability to transpose the dialect in "The Fisherman and His Wife" to "masterly control of a very simple colloquial style" (Crouch, 53). Crouch compares Gág's opening lines in this story with the translations by Edgar Taylor and Lucy Crane, and concludes that Gág possessed the more "sensitive ear" (Crouch, 53).

Gág also received a negative review. The critic for the *Boston Transcript* writes that Gág's illustrations fail to convey "North German eeriness"; moreover, he concludes that Gág retains "very little of the poetry of the stories themselves. The comic and grotesque is over-emphasized, and the pictures remind one far too often of the facetious art of Dr. Seuss."[21] Some reviewers mistakenly identified Gág's ink drawings as woodcuts.

Tales from Grimm is one of the most accessible editions of Grimm for children because Gág's story selections are from the most familiar and popular of the German fairy tales. She also succeeded in her goal to write smoothly and clearly. Her choice of words and her line drawings make it possible for younger children to grasp the subtleties of the story. Moreover, wider than usual space between the lines of type motivates younger children to read the book.

To publicize her book, Gág traveled to Cleveland in October and to Marshall Field's in Chicago and Wilmington, Delaware, in November. She exhausted herself during the "Ballyhoo Trip West" and was "not feeling up to snuff" even as late as the following February (Gág to Newton, 1 January 1937, CLRC).

Despite the general popularity of the Grimm volume, publisher Thomas Coward advised Gág against going to the Newbery Award announcement event in 1937. He predicted that the award committee would by-pass the book, and Dobbs quoted him as saying, "they won't

give the medal to Grimm, anyway—or to anything really worth while—
so why should we put ourselves out for them!" (Dobbs to Gág, 8 May
1937, CLRC). Nonetheless, Gág's editor retained a hopeful attitude.
Dobbs typed and sent to Gág the statements the committee members
had made publicly about the book. Among the speakers for the
Children's Book Week Program in New York City were Wanda Gág,
Ruth Sawyer, both storyteller and author, and Frederic G. Melcher, the
man who helped found both the Book Week and the Newbery Award.
The coveted Newbery Award proved elusive once again; and even the six
Honor Books excluded Gág's Grimm. Gág's platform companion Ruth
Sawyer won the accolade for her *Roller Skates*.[22] The somewhat autobio-
graphical story about a girl named Lucinda in New York City was edited
by May Massee, who had earlier approached Gág about doing a book for
Viking Press. First Lady Eleanor Roosevelt's attendance at the 1937 ban-
quet ceremony was evidence of the growing importance of the Newbery
Award.

In England, the book received favorable notice. Faber and Faber produced Gág's *Tales from Grimm* the following year, and reviewers for the
Times (London), *Irish News,* and other publications acclaimed it. For the
Observer, Humbert Wolfe wrote about the translation rather than the
illustrations, noting, "From the first page it was clear that Miss Gág was
chopping away a perfect brushwood of clumsy phraseology to let in the
light."[23] An unidentified reviewer for the British *Junior Bookshelf* notes
that the "prose is simple in construction, but flows smoothly; the solid
peasant nature of the originals is well presented and there is humor."
Perhaps the highest praise came in the statement that "with this new
translation we have gone back nearer the spirit of Grimm than our previous translations have taken us."[24]

Coward wanted to protect the potential sales of *Tales from Grimm* and
cautioned against the reprinting of a single story in magazines, such as
Child Life, for which Gág had arranged a reprinting of *Gone Is Gone*
under another title. Several years later, Gág initiated the possibility of a
magazine publishing "The Cat and Mouse Keep House," the second
fairy tale in her collection, but this never materialized.

Fairy tales held her attention. In 1937, Gág made a zinc plate for lithograph closest to her children's books—"Fairy Story," sometimes titled
"Fairy Tale." She tried it first on stone, but abandoned the medium.
Close to the center of the composition a seated girl with patches on her
clothes similar to Cinderella in *Tales from Grimm,* but wearing a scintillating crown, greets flying birds patterned after those in *The Funny Thing.*

Three dwarfs with the tall hats used for the endpiece the next year for *Snow White and the Seven Dwarfs* lean out of a cave to peer at three rabbits similar to *The ABC Bunny*. Stairs lead up the hill to the right and a rooster weathervane sits atop the single building. Flowers in the foreground and light, potato-like clouds contrast with the dark groomed hills. Gág also tried ideas for an "ABC Fight" book for the pacifist magazine, *Fight*. At the time she didn't feel like drawing in pen and ink; and shortly thereafter the world was at war again, which rendered the proposition moot. A "book-less" year passed in 1937, but Gág discussed the possibility of a forthcoming book of one hundred cat drawings with her publisher. They wanted to capitalize on the year 1938 being the tenth anniversary year for both Coward-McCann as a publishing company and Gág's *Millions of Cats*. Gág realized that she should not complete a new task hurriedly and noted that combining the cat with other subjects would be a mistake (Gág to Zigrosser, 23 March 1938, VP). Instead, she started work on another Brothers Grimm fairy tale.

Snow White and the Seven Dwarfs

It was no coincidence that Gág's *Snow White and the Seven Dwarfs* appeared in 1938. Walt Disney had released his full-length animated cartoon of the same classic fairy tale during Christmas vacation in 1937. Many children's librarians felt the Disney version was inaccurate and wanted to set the record straight. They knew the impact of moving pictures on the public; even in 1930, 100 million Americans went to the movies every week. Walt Disney Studio's previous successes had featured his own creations, such as Mickey Mouse and Donald Duck, but he then sought an appropriate classic fairy tale for a full-length cartoon.

Disney recalled the ambience of fairy-tale-like surroundings in Europe during World War I while he had served as a Red Cross driver in Strasbourg. When he traveled to Paris to receive a League of Nations medal for Mickey Mouse, the animated cartoon director extended his trip to include England, Holland, Italy, and Switzerland. He purchased a selection of children's books, especially those with illustrations of miniature people and creatures. Disney decided that the next film should be *Snow White,* and he embarked on the project with intensity.

European immigrants Albert Hurter and Gustaf Tenggren made preliminary sketches for the forthcoming film. Conferences dominated the working days, culminating in a "storyboard meeting" 24 November 1936. Despite objections from his staff, Disney invested substantial time

and energy in developing unique images for the seven dwarfs and insisted
that each dwarf be individualized in the film. With final decisions of
changing "Jumpy" to "Sneezy" and naming the previously unidentified,
dim-witted mute dwarf "Dopey," Disney completed the contingent of
seven. Because what some called "Disney's Folly" cost three times the bud-
geted amount of $500,000, some potential financiers feared bankruptcy
and withdrew funds. But W. G. Van Schmus, the New York manager of
the nation's largest movie theater, Radio City Music Hall, visited Hollywood to monitor the movie's progress. He booked it for the Christmas holidays, and the movie became an immediate box-office success.

The movie and the books emanating from the movie changed and
distorted the Brothers Grimm fairy-tale text considerably. Disney variants included the queen's behavior and disguises, the dwarfs, and the
deletion of important episodes. In the original fairy tale, for example, the
wicked queen orders the royal huntsman to kill Snow White. When the
huntsman returns with the heart of a wild pig, the Queen mistakes it for
the child's heart and orders it cooked; then she eats it. In the Disney version, the stepmother first banishes Snow White to the servants' quarters.
Later, the huntsman kills a small animal and gives the heart to the
wicked queen.

The royal stepmother in the fairy tale uses three distinct disguises, two
as an old woman and one as a peasant woman. In the movie, however, she
uses only one disguise. Similarly, in the fairy tale she tempts Snow White
with three different articles—bodice laces, which she pulls too tightly on
Snow White, a poisonous comb, and a poisoned apple. Disney, however,
limits the traditional three temptations to only one, the apple.

The dwarfs in the original story are generic, clean, tidy creatures. But
the seven Disney dwarfs are each unique in appearance; and their
names—Doc, Happy, Sneezy, Dopey, Grumpy, Bashful, and Sleepy—
describe their dispositions. Moreover, in the movie a bird guides Snow
White to their house, where she finds unwashed dishes in the sink, dirty
little shirts, wrinkled trousers, and a blanket of dust over the household.

Certain events in the story are also changed in the film. Concluding
that Snow White is dead, the dwarfs in the fairy tale place her in a crys-
tal casket. A traveling prince sees the beautiful woman and wants to
take the casket home. As the dwarfs jar the casket, the piece of poisoned
apple is dislodged from Snow White's throat and she wakes up. The
Prince then asks her to be his bride. In the Disney version, however,
"Love's First Kiss" reawakens her from sleeping death. While in the
original story the wicked stepmother dances to her death in red-hot

shoes, the Disney version concludes with the dwarfs chasing the step-mother into a bottomless pit, where she disappears forever.

Meanwhile, of more concern to librarians than even the film were the books on the market authorized by the Disney Studio and based on the plot and characters in the movie. Walt Disney Enterprises produced a twenty-page version with the title, *Walt Disney's Famous Seven Dwarfs,*[25] while the Whitman Publishing Company in Racine, Wisconsin, published an eleven-page book with the same title.[26] (Whitman's books, including those based on the Walt Disney films, sold in chain stores at inexpensive prices as a mass-market venture.) Two other variants shared the title *Walt Disney's Snow White and the Seven Dwarfs.* The Walt Disney Enterprises edition consisted of fifteen pages and the Whitman ninety-four.[27] A third Whitman "authorized version," *The Story of Walt Disney's Snow White and the Seven Dwarfs,* was 280 pages.[28]

Despite a preponderance of rave reviews of the movie in the media, most children's librarians and book reviewers responded negatively to the movie and the accompanying Disney books. These editions dismayed some librarians because Disney took so many liberties with the story. He infuriated Moore, who used all three of her powerful roles—as head of children's work at the New York Public Library, board member of the prestigious *Horn Book,* and reviewer for the *New York Herald Tribune Books*—to make scathing remarks about the Disney books. Moore wrote, "The saddest publication of 1937 . . . was the Snow White from Hollywood. It smelt quite as bad as it looked and provides a striking example of the let's have fun with anything we can use in our business state of mind. . . . The acceptance in book form of such a substitute for the lovely old fairy tale of Snow White calls for sharp critical comment."[29] She not only wrote negative reviews but actively sought a correct version of the fairy tale for children, and Wanda Gág was the logical choice. Gág's *Tales from Grimm,* published only two years earlier, was familiar to readers, but "Snow White" was not part of that volume. Moore personally pressured Coward-McCann to have Wanda Gág produce a version of the fairy tale.

By March 1937, Gág had responded to Moore's prodding by completing her translation. Her text paralleled the Grimm Brothers' version, in contrast to the Disney rendition. She retained the gruesome episode of the stepmother eating what she thought was the cooked heart of Snow White. Gág also used the traditional stepmother's three disguises and the three temptations. A "peddler woman" enticed with bodice laces, an "old woman" tempted with a comb, and a "peasant woman" offered an apple to Snow White. While in an earlier draft the stepmother "asked" the royal huntsman to dispose of Snow White, in the later version she "told" him to, which is an interpretation closer to the original German. Gág polished her version by substituting "ebon" for "ebony" in one sentence and by changing "you are" to "thou art" in another. She explored distinctions in the dwarfs' beds—"hard, soft, short, narrow, flat, fluffy, right"—and settled on "high, deep, low, steep, lumpy, bumpy, right." In notebooks, Gág had made lists of rhyming words—"do, through, to, two, wood, you, blue, dew, hue, knew, new, rue, true, . . . adieu"—to incorporate in the verses. Humphreys critiqued her manuscript and suggested changes, such as the sequence of sentences describing the birth of Snow White, and referred Gág to the *Collegiate Dictionary* to find alternative words. Penciled notes, such as "Flops [Flavia] discuss with me" indicate that Gág also sought advice from other readers of the manuscript (manuscript for *Snow White,* CLRC).

It was in this context that Gág offered her translation in March 1938 to Bruce Gould, the editor at *Ladies Home Journal.* Gág notes, "since the Walt Disney version seems to be causing considerable controversy both in England and in this country, it occurred to me that it might be interesting to present an actual translation for comparison." She adds that she had not yet seen the movie. The editor rebuffed her overture. On the carbon copy of her letter to the woman's magazine, Gág wrote in pencil, "They didn't want it" (Gág to Gould, 3 March 1938, CLRC).

While Gág respected the Brothers Grimm text, she made the story more accessible to children by modifying it slightly without changing the action. Translating closely to the German, she consistently used the term "Queen" for the king's second wife rather than the term "Stepmother" found in some nineteenth-century translations. She substituted "heart" for the original "lung and liver" that the wicked woman ate. Gág retained familiar words associated with the fairy tale, such as "fairest," but avoided words used in earlier editions, such as "beseech." Snow White's response to the disguised stepmother could be translated as "I dare not take anything," but Gág wrote: "I'm not allowed to take anything from strangers" (*Snow White,* 34).

Gág used parallel structure for the dwarfs discovering that someone had disturbed their table and beds. The original lacks description, but Gág individualized each bed—"it's all humped up and crumpled . . . It's full of wrinkles . . . It's full of crinkles" (*Snow White,* 19). She eliminated the seventh dwarf's sleeping with each of the others for one hour a night. Gág also retained the prominence of the number seven referring to dwarfs, beds, and hills. Knowing that children count carefully, Gág explained in the text that only six dwarfs went off to work, for they took turns to stay with the casket. She provided rhymed phrases besides the familiar "Mirror, Mirror, on the wall, Who's the fairest one of all?" Gág commented that "It would have been better" for the queen to have stayed away from Snow White's wedding. Rather than concluding the book with the queen dancing in red-hot shoes until she fell down dead, Gág modified the ending in two ways. The queen "was given a pair of red hot shoes with which she had to dance out her wicked life"; the final sentence notes that all the others "lived happily ever after" (*Snow White*, 43). The artist used adjectives for the colors, "rosy red" and "ebon black." The wicked queen "turned green and yellow" in the original text, but not "purple with rage" (*Snow White*, 43). Gág never claimed to translate literally, and the title page reiterates the disclaimer "freely translated and illustrated." Not one of her variations is intrusive, but rather interprets and enhances the text, resulting in one of the better contemporary American editions.

Rose Dobbs responded to the 3,417-word manuscript in April. She considered the proposed first line too long and the word "wonderment" and phrase "Sweet innocent" too mannered and sentimental. The editor also shared a personal concern. "Another thing that has always bothered me in connection with any version of this story is this: how did the drops of blood fall on the snow? Was the window open? If so, would the Queen be apt to sew before an open window in the middle of winter?" (Dobbs to Gág, 8 April 1938, CLRC). Both the Grimm version and Gág's translation leave the matter unexplained.

With the text completed, Gág then worked on the illustrations. She hoped to complete them before spring, when she wanted to work outside. Gág individualized the beds in early sketches, drawing each according to the appropriate adjective, such as "high" or "lumpy," but the final ink illustration has uniform beds. In illustrations as well as in the manuscript, she interpreted the dwarfs' lifestyle as neat and clean. No Disney-type embellishments, such as food-covered dishes in the sink, dust on the furniture, or dirty shirts and wrinkled trousers awaiting Snow White as laundress existed in the Gág version. Gág did draw details such as slippers under the bed and nightshirts hung in an orderly fashion.

Gág considered dedicating the book to Moore, or at least inviting her to write an introduction, but ultimately concurred with Dobbs's belief that there should be "no hint that the book was a result of pressure from librarians" (Dobbs to Gág, 11 April 1938, CLRC). Instead, they merely informed Moore that Gág was making progress on the book and in late April sent her the galley proofs, hoping for a prepublication review. Pressure bore down on Gág, and she completed the final illustrations by late April. Gág wrote to her friend Alma Scott, to whose children Pat and Janey she dedicated the book, "My Snow White is all finished. I did it in seven weeks. Some rush" (Gág to Scott, 11 May 1938, CLRC).

Two illustrations, the infant Snow White and the dwarfs' discovery of her asleep later in the story, appeared in the Coward-McCann house organ, *Three Star Final.* Dobbs "took the whole lot over to Miss Moore yesterday, and you should have seen me trotting after her as she rushed from department to department all over the [New York Public] library showing them" (Dobbs to Gág, 27 April 1938, CLRC). Moore telegraphed the *Horn Book* staff in Boston to hold the press until they received an illustration to accompany her review. Both Dobbs and Moore especially liked the arrangement of the seven dwarfs on the title page.

The published book was forty-four pages long and sold for $1. Moore's review in the combined May and June issue of *Horn Book* preceded other critiques and avoided direct reference to the Disney version. Unusually early for a fall book, Gág's *Snow White and the Seven Dwarfs* was published 8 August 1938. The dust jacket copy quoted from the *Horn Book* review, which states: "It will be good news to many readers that Wanda Gág has made her own translation and pictures for *Snow White and the Seven Dwarfs.* . . . The story is as satisfyingly told in pictures as it is in the words of the text. In both there is a childlike simplicity united with great strength and beauty. The inimitable drawings of the dwarfs restore their true character as dwarfs."[30] Louise Bechtel, who had perused Gág's portfolio and rejected her as a potential illustrator a decade earlier, compared Gág's book with Disney's. She contrasted his "over-elaborated story" and the "big-nosed heroes" to her "simplicity." The black-and-white illustrations have "just enough magic and fear . . . their humor and detail are a stimulus to the imagination."[31]

It was inevitable that Gág's *Snow White and the Seven Dwarfs* would be compared with the Disney interpretation in the American press. Gág's book initially fared better than Disney's. Eaton, in reviewing the book for the *New York Times,* wrote, "Wanda Gág's own translation, illustrated by her inimitable drawings, is an event and a particularly welcome one in a year when thousands of people, young and old, have been made Snow White conscious."[32] May Lamberton Becker commented, "When I reflect upon the stationary pictures in color spread over the country in books that were by-products of the film, I am sure that lovers of children and good books will do well to keep Miss Gág's at hand and let it do its work in the establishment of standards of good taste."[33] The only negative comments were about the poor paper binding; consequently, Coward-McCann bound the October press run in cloth.

Snow White and the Seven Dwarfs was one of five Honor Books when Thomas Handforth's *Mei Li* won the 1939 Caldecott Award. Elizabeth Enright won the 1939 Newbery Award for *Thimble Summer* along with five Honor Books.[34] Faber and Faber issued the book in September 1938 in Great Britain. Eleanor Graham mentioned it casually along with the Disney version in her feature article, "The Season's Children's Books, Great Richness and Variety" in *Bookseller.*[35] The same issue announced the publication of Gág's *Snow White* and *the Seven Dwarfs.*[36]

British critics reviewed the book more harshly than the American. Englishman G. Bell, reviewing for the *New Statesman* and *Nation,* stated that the black-and-white illustrations had "nothing very special about them, though no doubt they will look rather fine when the little ones have spent a wet afternoon chalking them over."[37] Writing almost twenty-five years later, Marcus S. Crouch stated that the book was not in Wanda Gág's "best vein" and that it was "hurried out," "showed signs of haste," and was "over-full of those cliches which come in handy when inspiration flags" (Crouch, 53).

Gág refused to travel west to promote *Snow White and the Seven Dwarfs,* but she agreed to speak at a few events. On 19 November 1938 she gave three identical presentations for different audiences at the Illustrator's Forum at Wannamaker's Children's Book Fair. The New York Public Library's expert in storytelling, Mary Gould Davis, presided over the three sessions, introducing guests Gág, Kurt Wiese, and James McDonald. In addition, Moore invited Gág to speak at a New York Public Library gathering. Dobbs advised her to talk about fairy tales, but to avoid any direct criticism of Disney. Later that month Bertha Miller, editor of *Horn Book,* telegraphed Dobbs to request "the fairy tale paper" for the journal. Since she offered no payment, Gág insisted that she herself retain copyright and added, "A little money would be acceptable and . . . you shall be remembered with a picture." Gág polished her manuscript, which became a feature article, "I Like Fairy Tales." Because of policy, *Horn Book* paid no fee and copyrighted the entire spring issue in its name.

Coward-McCann celebrated its tenth anniversary in 1938, as did Wanda Gág's first book. Gág designed a slender wrap-around strip with a birthday cake motif to use for promoting *Millions of Cats.* Now that Gág had finished the Brothers Grimm translations and illustrations, she turned to fine art and completed a print. Cats were the subject of discussion about a book at the beginning of the year, but became the seven cats arranged in

one important lithograph on zinc, "Siesta." A jury selected it for the New
York's World's Fair "American Art Today" exhibition.

She was adamant, however, in her refusal to undertake other children's
book assignments for 1939. Gág reiterated her policy of alternating projects. She wrote to a friend that she would not do a book in the forthcoming year, for "the other side of me is clamoring for expression, and it is
taking the form of painting" (Gág to Newton, October 1939, CLRC).
Dorothy M. Bryan at Dodd, Mead and Company invited Gág to illustrate
a collection of Danish fairy tales compiled by Ruth Bryan Owen (Dorothy
Bryan to Gág, 19 October 1938, CLRC).[38] As usual, Gág refused; the
company then hired artist Marc Simont, who received the Caldecott
Award in 1957 for another book. Then Helen Dean Fish at Frederick A.
Stokes proposed that Gág illustrate a book jacket, a wrap-around, and
twenty spot drawings (Fish to Gág, 14 November 1939, CLRC). That
company had rejected Humphreys' overture for "Funny Fairy Tales" on
behalf of Gág almost fifteen years earlier, and now Gág declined.

On the Home Front

Meanwhile, a Gág Family Show traveled around the country from 1936
to 1938. Tyler McWhorter, organizer of a touring exhibit, was the same
"Uncle Mac" who managed the St. Paul Institute of Art and Sciences Gág
had attended more than twenty years before. The exhibit represented
artistic endeavors by all seven Gag siblings, such as book illustrations by
Wanda and Flavia and *Sue Sew and Sew* by the three sisters. Photographs
taken of their father's murals in New Ulm and a watercolor entitled
"Down at Grandma's" by their uncle Joseph Biebl conveyed a sense of
their artistic roots. Contemporary photographs taken at All Creation,
including one of the cat Snoopy, updated the viewers on the lives of the
Gag family. California sites for the show included Beverly Hills and
Pasadena; the Los Angeles Public Library displayed the show during the
American Library Association conference of 1937. Then it moved to the
Minnesota cities of New Ulm, Winona, and St. Paul. When Wanda Gág
heard that it might go to the College of Saint Catherine in St. Paul, she
wrote to Alma Scott, "We heathen Gags do get into the most unexpect-
ed places" (Gág to Scott, 11 May 1938, CLRC).

Desiring to paint, Gág pursued another plan during 1938; it was the
year she contemplated a Guggenheim Fellowship. When asking Lewis
Mumford for a letter of recommendation, she drafted, "I have long wanted
to take a year off from bread and butter activities (that is, juvenile books)

to satisfy an increasing urge to work in color and to carry out various theories and ideas which have been piling up within me for the last five or six years" (Gág to Mumford, 12 October 1938, CLRC).

In the application itself, she qualified this position, adding, "I have never regarded [juvenile writing] as hack work and have always put as much of myself into it as I would into a print or a painting. However, it is an outlet for only one side of myself." Gág continued that she had "been by necessity restricted by a relatively small section of the American Scene. Because of this I have long wished for the opportunity to travel to other parts of the United States, and to record my reactions in a form which would be at the same time a document, a comment, and a work of art" (in CLRC).

Her fellowship proposal was entitled "Creative Work in Painting in the United States." The Guggenheim Fellowship parameters stated that the fellowships are open to men or women, married or unmarried, normally twenty-five to forty years old. Wanda Gág was forty-five when she applied in October. Gág's own selection of books to submit with the application were *Snippy and Snappy, The ABC Bunny,* and *Tales from Grimm.* She also enclosed seven watercolors, seven drawings, eleven lithographs, and five woodcuts. As mentioned in chapter 1, the committee selected five awardees, including Dehn and Zigrosser, but no woman. Gág did not express resentment about her rejection and in the aftermath even questioned her ability to meet the expectations of the grant at that time. Zigrosser's proposed study of contemporary American graphic arts, its background and its relation to modern life, resulted in a publication, *The Artist in America,* which devoted one of its twenty-four chapters to Gág.

In a reflective essay written in 1940, Gág acknowledged that she had spent most of her time during the prior ten years on juvenile books. Yet she tried to maintain some balance in pursuing her interests. While in the Guggenheim application Gág had sought support for painting, she nevertheless could not abandon her growing interest in writing. Gág continued to work in other fields, too, commenting, "it is important to guard against a narrow viewpoint." Gág maintained a consistent attitude toward all her projects, however, and that was to do her best. "The only way I can enjoy doing a piece of work is to keep on re-drawing, re-writing or re-constructing it until I know that I, at least, can't do it any better be her."[39]

Chapter Five

...Wanda Will Have to Finish: The 1940s

True to her principle of challenging herself with new ventures, Gág launched several projects related to children's literature during the last six years of her life. She created an unusual autobiography—*Growing Pains,* which consists of excerpts from her adolescent and early adult diaries and concludes with her leaving Minnesota for New York City—and one last picture book—*Nothing at All,* for which she learned to handle the color separations with lithography for three colors. Then she finalized two illustrated collections of her Brothers Grimm fairy-tale translations. And she translated and illustrated thirty-five more fairy tales for *Three Gay Tales* and the posthumously published *More Tales from Grimm.* Gág also acknowledged that she enjoyed the writing process as much as the artistic process. Gág revamped her stories for the radio and also wrote several manuscripts that remain unpublished. During the same time frame, the fine art world further acknowledged her importance when the Metropolitan Museum of Art and the Library of Congress each acquired Gág's prints as "purchase prizes" for their permanent collections.

Growing Pains

Politically, the decade of the 1940s opened with a sense of impending doom in both Europe and Asia. America intended to remain neutral, despite the aggression of Fascists Adolf Hitler in Germany and Benito Mussolini in Italy. Meanwhile, Japanese militants gained power and invaded China. When the Nazis invaded Poland in 1939, Great Britain and France declared war on Germany. The United States later joined these Allied forces and soon fought on three fronts. Against this threatening backdrop, Gág concluded work on her "kid diaries," which revived memories of a more peaceful time in a midwestern village and in the Twin Cities of Minneapolis and St. Paul. Her progress on the autobiography was kept a secret from her editor for years (Gág to Flavia Gag,

16 November 1937, Harm). She cautioned Flavia, "This is to warn you not to mention the diaries to anyone . . . and especially not to Rose [Dobbs]. Don't forget yourself and say, 'Lucky I have some typing to do for Wanda.'"

A few notable artists are known for keeping a journal or corresponding faithfully on a daily basis. One was her contemporary Paul Klee, who kept a diary that was published as *Tagebucher von Paul Klee* (Diary of Paul Klee) a decade after Gág's death.[1] Gág acquainted herself with diaries by other authors and artists. In the 1920s, Gág had read Anatole France's *Little Pierre*, filled with anecdotes about his childhood but written when he was an adult (Gág to Larrabee, 24 September [1923?], CLRC). Gág knew both Delacroix's journal and *The Letters of Van Gogh to His Brother* (Diary, 14 March 1938). Gág's consistent diary keeping as a teenage artist seemed unusual among friends she consulted. Her best childhood friend, however, Alma Schmidt, made daily diary entries on her visits to Governor Eberhart's home in St. Paul. From the age of fifteen, Gág wrote in her journal almost daily and continued this routine. As an adult, Gág resisted the temptation to destroy the diaries; she now considered them valuable as evidence of the development of an artist.

For years, Gág had considered how she might write an autobiography; Coward-McCann had offered her $1,000 for one immediately after the success of *Millions of Cats*. Coward-McCann was not the only publisher interested in such a publication. In 1929, Harrison Smith of the firm Jonathan Cape and Harrison Smith, had inquired about the possibility of publishing Gág's journals (Smith to Gág, 19 January 1929, CLRC). The publishing company, which had learned that Gág kept a diary from critic Lewis Gannett, had earlier declined an offer for another Gág project. But Gág had declined both publishers' offers, responding that she wanted to produce an autobiography in her own way and on her own schedule. Moreover, the publishing business was not good after the stock market crash of 1929.

Gág envisioned her youthful diaries as the basis for an autobiography. She realized that transcribing the diaries to manuscript form would be no easy task. Her shorthand would be difficult for anyone to read, and Gág herself had never mastered typing. Gág hired Flavia, who already typed her correspondence and knew her idiosyncrasies, to type a manuscript draft. The excerpts survived several stages of distillation. First, Gág marked portions of the diary entries for Flavia to type. Then she deleted some parts of the first typed draft herself, such as incidents which cast New Ulm citizens in a negative light. Some matters were too sensitive; for example, she did not mention her mother's alcoholism. Then Gág deliberately blurred some identities. In 1930 she gave her sister a list of pseudonyms to substitute for real names. For example, one of her youthful "cavaliers," Edgar Hermann, was now a medical doctor in Minnesota. She changed his name in the published diary to Armand Emraad, although their relationship during youth was "innocent beyond belief!" (Gág to Flavia Gag, 24 September 1930, CLRC). By 1939, Flavia had finished typing a manuscript draft. In March, Gág deleted portions for the third time, as it still remained too lengthy and unwieldy. The proposed manuscript for *Growing Pains* finally reached her publisher by February of the next year.

When publication with Coward-McCann seemed imminent, Gág corresponded with some of the people she mentioned in the diaries to obtain permission to use their names, both as a courtesy and a prevention against libel. In addition, she hoped that some friends had kept her youthful correspondence for keepsakes, such as sketches or illustrated cards. By recovering these items, she could compare her adult work with images she produced as a child.

Together with Rose Dobbs, Gág visualized the sections of the book. Zigrosser, who seemed the appropriate person to write the foreword, described Gág in context with other contemporary American graphic artists and stated that Gág exemplified courage in allowing herself to be "seen." Gág contributed a historical introduction, reviewing the background of her thirty-two individual diaries. Substantial excerpts from the diaries would be interspersed with graphics. A section of "Contrasts 1904–1938" juxtaposes her childhood drawings with her adult work. A "Who's Who in the Diary" identifies most people mentioned but also contains some pseudonyms. Gág dedicated the book to "My Mother and Father."

Coward-McCann hired free-lance editors, who reduced the typed pages to one-third of the original transcription. Nevertheless, the diary excerpts alone totaled 468 pages, with additional drawings and introductory and concluding matter. Thomas Coward struggled with manufacturing problems. He considered the cost estimate from a New York City printer too expensive and selected a cheaper one from outside the city.

Growing Pains is as multilayered as the author herself. Because the initial purpose of the diaries was to keep track of her finances, there is a record of her financial struggles. The first entry, "Monday, Oct. 12, 1908," notes that on that very day she sent a drawing to *Journal Junior* and a story with a picture to *McCall's Magazine* for possible publication. She recalls sending three articles to *Youth's Companion* previously and ponders,

"I wonder how the whole thing will turn out." She seems considerably younger than fifteen in the subsequent passage, in which she recalls that acquaintance "Martha Schmid didn't believe that I drew free hand. She thinks I trace. Trace indeed! When I don't even care much for copying" (*Growing*, 1). During this time Gág moved from adolescence to womanhood, and the book documents her growing awareness of herself alone and in relationships. While the first two parts of the book cover the everyday life of a high school student in the town of New Ulm, the latter four cover her art training while in the cities of St. Paul and Minneapolis. Reflective comments accompany the litany of activities described as Gág coped with life. Her maturing is evident in the diaries, but even the final entry, written when she was twenty-four, seems naive: "My Journal Man wrote and said that he had a room reserved at the Studio Club in New York for me. Happy, gee—" (*Growing*, 467). As she rereads letters from Dehn and her "former cavaliers," with the intention to discard some, she remarks "Funny world." The pivotal last sentence, an undated entry likely written at the end of September 1928, states, "Adolph [sic], Arnold Blanch and I start out for New York Wednesday evening" (*Growing*, 468), leaving room for an eventual sequel beginning with her arrival in New York City.

The publication date for *Growing Pains,* a 504-page book with illustrations, was 23 September 1940. Copies sold in bookstores for $3.75; the Coward-McCann sales force had advised against pricing the book at $5 because book sales across the country were in decline. As usual, autograph parties and reviews followed. The "Women of Tomorrow" radio-show hostess interviewed Gág in New York City a few weeks later, on 4 October. Gág then traveled to the *Boston Herald* book fair, to J. L. Hudson Company in Detroit, and to F. and R. Lazarus and Company in Columbus, Ohio (Cecil Goldbeck to Gág, 30 September 1940, CLRC). In November she journeyed to Halle Brothers Company in Cleveland and then to the Minneapolis Dayton's department store for autograph sessions. At the latter, not only did she autograph the recently published *Growing Pains* but also her first two books, *Millions of Cats* and *The Funny Thing,* both on the market more than ten years. Gág and "Armaand" in the diary renewed their acquaintance and had "some good laughs" over their youthful days (Gág to Hilda Growald, 14 November 1945, CLRC). This was to be her last trip to Minnesota.

Growing Pains prompted letters from professionals and friends, as well as reviews in both journals and newspapers. Della MacGregor, children's librarian at the St. Paul Public Library, sent a congratulatory letter to the publisher. Gladys English, from the Los Angeles Public Library, promised to review the book at a forthcoming regional library meeting. M. C. Scoggin in the *Library Journal,* Thomas Craven for the *New York Herald Tribune* book section, and Gannett for the *Boston Transcript* reached audiences new to Gág. Craven, as author of *The Treasury of American Prints,*[2] knew Gág's art, and had included her "Siesta" and "Grandma's Parlor" among the hundred selections in his book. He summarized in his *Tribune* review, "This book is not a conscious literary exercise; it is the unaffected account of the struggles of a girl who was determined to make herself an artist, and who succeeded nobly. Throughout the book the author's extraordinary purity of mind shines out. . . . She faced life, never whined, truckled, or hoped for miracles, and with enormous self-discipline, developed her capacities to the fullest extent."[3]

Moore wrote in the *Horn Book,* "I found the record so moving and so important at this time of storm and stress and great confusion regarding youth all over the world that it seems to me another proof of her intelligence and keen awareness of what youth has to give if left free to meet life on its own terms."[4] A reviewer for the *Boston Transcript* commented, "This is a most readable record of normal, wholesome development, told with the unspoiled untampered-with naivete of the most pathetic era of life. . . . Life is never again more serious or more definite."[5]

In many ways *Growing Pains* reads like a novel, with plot, characters, setting, theme, and mood. The plot is Gág's daily struggle toward becoming an artist. Her commitment to writing on a regular basis makes it possible for the excerpts from the diaries to achieve a continuity. Gág's best friends are the main characters, who change and become more interesting as they mature. Because Gág was candid in her youthful observations, the characters come to life. The time is 1908 to 1924, the setting her hometown of New Ulm in the first half of the book, the metropolitan Twin Cities of Minneapolis and St. Paul in the second. There is an interlude in Springfield, Minnesota. Gág's style is flowing and informal, touched up by the editing. The theme is her yearning to become an artist, en route setting priorities and managing time—universal problems in modern society. The mood is one of either jubilation or pathos, reminding readers of the joy and anguish of young adult life. The sorting out of her life is most poignant in the chapter "Myself and Many Me's."

Despite the good reviews, the prestigious literary awards again went to others. Armstrong Sperry received the Newbery Award for *Call to Courage; Growing Pains* did not qualify for the Caldecott Award. Moreover,

Growing Pains did not sell well. "I get loads of swell comments on *Growing Pains* but the re-orders come in very slowly," Dobbs confided to Gág. "Miss Moore mentioned you and the book especially at the opening of children's book week. She said it was a wonderful book" (Dobbs to Gág, 15 November 1940, CLRC). In contrast to Gág's books for children, *Growing Pains* was never published in Great Britain; the only overseas publisher to purchase the rights was Danish.

When the book was first published, correspondence inundated Gág. Humphreys organized the letters in files with labels, "People Who Want Her to Illustrate Their Books," "Friends," and "Business." Referring to the best-seller list from the *New York Herald Tribune* Sunday book section, George T. Dunlap wrote, "It irks me to see Hemingway getting almost a hundred percent vote in the fiction and *Growing Pains* not mentioned in the non-fiction" (Dunlap to Gág, 5 December 1940, CLRC). He continued his letter, written from Pinehurst, North Carolina, by inviting Gág to publish something similar for Grosset and Dunlap. Louise Raymond, at Harper and Brothers, asked if she would illustrate Richard Hughes's *Don't Blame Me* (Raymond to Gág, 8 April 1940, CLRC). When she refused, Fritz Eichenberg illustrated it for publication within the calendar year. Gág completely abandoned her "Blaa Book," in which she had pasted newspaper clippings and congratulatory letters. "I feel like going into 'hiding' for half a year so that I could do what I want, for a change" (Diary, 1 March 1941).

She let much of the incoming correspondence accumulate for a year. Then she drafted letters in response, which Humphreys and Flavia typed. Among those she appreciated most were letters from young girls who said that her book gave them courage to live with more conviction. A year after the book's publication, she jotted in her diary, "I continue to get very touching letters from young girls who have just finished reading *Growing Pains* who say that the book helped them to feel more at home with themselves, given them the courage to fight their art and life battles and so on" (Diary, 24 November 1941).

Gág had two ideas for continuing the autobiographical theme. One possibility was working on reminiscences about her home life prior to beginning her diary in 1908 (Gág to Raye Kirkman, 22 October 1941, CLRC). She worked on this intermittently for several years. Her other impulse was to edit the diaries covering her arrival and early years in New York City. Gág confided to her friends that she contemplated a sequel to *Growing Pains*. Only a year after she completed her work on the published autobiography, Gág took five or six diaries out of her safety deposit box at the bank to review. She made orange dots in the margin to indicate potentially useful material. Eventually she concluded that they dealt primarily with her relationship with Adolf Dehn and lacked substance of interest to the public.

Gág then considered another kind of publication covering the years 1917 to 1929, alternating diary entries with letters to and from her family and acquaintances, especially Adolf Dehn. His letters from that early period described his serving in the army as a conscientious objector. But because he, too, had gained considerable fame as an artist by 1941, Gág wondered if he might publish the letters himself.

She wrote in her diary only sporadically in the late 1930s and for some years neglected it completely, merely recalling and summarizing her life every now and then. Ultimately, neither the story of her childhood nor the sequel to her published diary materialized. She died before bringing either to fruition, and the executors of her estate deposited all the diaries with Zigrosser, now at the Philadelphia Museum of Art. As in the diaries of her youth, Gág continued to make candid commentary about individuals and events; some of these individuals had become renowned. Family members had access to the diaries; Flavia Gag made notes from them for a possible biography about her sister. It was never published.

Less than a month following the publication of *Growing Pains,* the Weyhe Gallery hosted a retrospective show from 12–31 October 1940 entitled "Wanda Gág: 35 Years of Picture Making." The invitation featured Gág's self-portrait: she is wearing a bathing suit, along with visor hat to protect her from the sun, and is engaged in her favorite activity—drawing. In the foreground lies a book by the Brothers Grimm. Gág used variants of this image for other purposes, such as on holiday greeting cards.

An exhibit at the University of Minnesota later that fall, curated by Ruth Laurence, proved unprofitable for Gág; no prints sold. At the Philadelphia Art Alliance's "Exhibition of Living Lithography," Gág received a Certificate of Merit for Distinguished Work in the Art of Lithography.

Nothing at All

In the 1940s, Gág realized that despite her neglect of her diary from February 1939 to March 1942, she was increasingly interested in writing stories. Fifteen years earlier, Gág had written a story entitled "Nothing at All" and later had scribbled on the cover of a small memorandum notebook, "inception of Nothing At All while we were still at Tumble

Timbers; Batik notes in here, therefore about 1926" (CLRC). Now she revived the idea as the basis for her next book. She drafted a letter to a fan, presumably for Flavia or Humphreys to type, writing, "a little dog who has been at the back of my mind for years insisted on getting herself notarized" (Gág to a Mr. Motley, 22 October 1941, handwritten draft, CLRC).

On 11 March 1941 Gág celebrated her forty-eighth birthday in New York City without her usual birthday companion, Zigrosser. Conscious that both of her parents had died in their late forties, she considered this an especially significant birthday; she had feared that she might not live to the same age. Moreover, when her prints and drawings reaped only $250 in 1940, she was ready to modify her alternate year schedule and embark on another children's book project in 1941. "Well, could I help it if Nothing-At-All (that little invisible dog who has been trying to get me to make him into a story for years and years) suddenly popped up again in my mind and got himself jelled at last?" (Diary, 11 March 1941).

Details changed from the holograph stage to the printed book, but the basic story line remained substantially the same through several revisions. In the draft the invisible dog cried, while the published text states, "But do you think he sat down and cried? Oh no—he had a plan" (CLRC). This reference to "a plan" reiterates Gág's management principle. Journalist Anne Herendeen noted Gág's use of the word "plan" when she interviewed Gág for an article in the *Century* (Herendeen, 427) more than a dozen years earlier. And Bobo, the man of the mountain in her second book, *The Funny Thing,* also had made a "plan" to prevent the "aminal" from eating dolls.

In *Nothing at All,* characters, plot, and setting differ from her previous original texts. This time she introduces six characters—three dogs (including an invisible one), two children, and a jackdaw bird. Lewis Gannett read an early draft and suggested that she substitute another creature for the magician squirrel, so she changed it to a bird. Each dog lives contentedly in a uniquely designed doghouse. One day, a girl and a boy each choose a dog to take home; they do not see the invisible third dog. Therefore, it yearns to become visible, and the jackdaw bird offers to coach him. By following a prescribed ritual and working hard, the dog acquires a shape and visibility.

While Gág's first three picture books contain both outdoor and indoor scenes, *Nothing at All* takes place entirely in the open rural country. Gág discarded earlier ideas for the setting, such as "In a forest," "clustered Hill Country," "Tumble Timbers," and "far off land of Jimble Jamble."

Interestingly, rhythmic and alliterated text describes the final surroundings—"They lived in a far forgotten corner of an old forgotten farm in
three forgotten kennels which stood there in a row" (*Nothing*).
Gág's characteristic rhythm and repetition permeate the text.
Rhyming words such as "ought, bought, caught, thought, fought"
appeared on lists and were later abandoned. "Oh birds and bugs! Oh
jiggy jobs!" didn't survive long under Gág's scrutiny. Lines ending in
"tall," "small," and "all" change as the story develops. Gág added the
concepts of "orphan" and "adopted" at the last minute. The jackdaw
teaches the invisible dog the phrase, "I'm busy getting dizzy," which
becomes the repeated incantation. Both text and illustration exemplify
clarity, as the story moves logically from one episode to the next.

Refusing to repeat herself by using pen and ink medium, she chose
lithography. Moreover, since she had made lithographs for *The ABC
Bunny,* Gág added another dimension—color. Her editor suggested a
prototype for a three-color book with shades of red and green to accompany the black base lines, namely Tibor Gergeley's illustrations for *True
Monkey Stories.*[6] Gág explained, "It's a medium I've never tried before
although it's sufficiently like lithography to make it partly familiar. Do
you remember those ground glass plates we used to have as children?
One could trace pictures through them, with a pencil. I use a finely
grained glass with a 9H lead pencil. . . . The result is like a fine crayon
drawing, and since I am using black and two colors, I hope we'll get a
really attractive job" (Gág to Howard Gag, 6 April 1941, CLRC). To
accomplish the task, she installed a florescent light under a glass-covered
work table. In contrast to the lithographic process used for *The ABC
Bunny,* she could erase and draw finer lines. She had to make three plates
for color—red, green, and black—for each page. With the light table
she could lay the plate on top of the base drawing.

Not only did Gág try another medium, but she drew differently as
well. During the summer of 1939 she developed a new way of observing
shapes, using the terms "facets" and "meridians" to describe them. She
evolved the first step of this construction method to interpret three-
dimensional objects on 23 October 1928 and the second in July 1939.
Gág considered her approach different from the cubists, who broke
down forms, "while mine is building up forms. Once more I live in a
world of my own construction, within self-created, compactly felt sym-
bols. Again I am drawing from within to without" (Diary, 2 August
1939). She used this new insight for drawing the tree trunk and the aer-
ial view of plant beds for her forthcoming book.

During this year, Gág used studies and drawings made in the late 1920s for lithographs on zinc plates, "Macy's Stairway" and "Barns at Glen Gardner." She did not look back, however, at her trio of picture books from 1928 to 1931 when she used the double-page spread. In contrast, she used only one in *Nothing at All* for a scene in which the invisible dog scampers around as the children transport the kennels. The outcome is less impressive than the earlier books. This last picture book is more similar to an illustrated book. In only a few illustrations does the action move from the left to right to encourage page-turning, and some images remain static. Cookie-cutter endpaper and dedication-page illustrations seem trite.

Gág drew from ten to fourteen hours a day to meet the deadline. She left mail unanswered and her clothes and apartment in a mess. Gág's brother encouraged her to take a break and attend the American Artists Congress. He admonished, "I don't see how you can keep up that grind day after day the way you have been doing" (Howard Gag to Gág, "April to May" 1941, CLRC). She recalled the concept of a Finnish word, *sisu*, meaning patience and strong will without passion—"it comes to me miraculously in times of stress. It sounds to me like what I've always referred to when I've said 'There are times when it is necessary to do the impossible.' Any Gag knows that this can be done!" (Diary, 18 August 1941).

While under the pressure of the nearing deadline, Gág suffered from a rash on her hands. She thought it might have resulted from any number of causes—poison ivy, wood allergy, reaction from rayon curtains, or food poisoning. The condition handicapped her drawing. To provide some relief, she tied six or seven fingers in rags, which limited her ability to draw delicate lines and shadings. While her book was about a dog getting busy being dizzy, the artist herself complained about dizziness. A doctor friend, Hugh Darby, suspected the cause to be lead poisoning from the pencils she sharpened on sandpaper.

Meanwhile, Howard Gag labored over the hand-lettering of the text. His last effort had been in 1933, for *The ABC Bunny,* and he had lost his touch in the interim. Gág admonished him to keep the letters "e, "k," and "w" open. For his labors, Coward-McCann paid Howard $150 rather than the $100 he had received for earlier books. While Gág had dedicated that last picture book, *The ABC Bunny,* to her only nephew, she dedicated *Nothing at All* to her only niece, two-year-old Barbara Jean. The child was the daughter of Asta, the fourth oldest Gag sibling, and Herbert Treat.

Gág was nervous about the results of her first book in color. Because she drew all three plates in black, it was difficult to predict the outcome when the colored inks were superimposed on the paper. In the next production stage, plates were etched from the lithographs for each of the three colors: black, red, and green. "We pulled proofs and thanks to goodness, they were all I could wish for—they looked grand" (Diary, 18 August 1941). Printer William C. D. Glaser sent a set of color proofs to Gág in early May. Glaser and his wife, Lillian, printed the book after making impressions on transfer paper. This guaranteed the lighter shade of red that Gág wanted. Dobbs cautioned Gág to have realistic expectations. She predicted the inevitability of a slight coarsening of color resulting from printing by power machines rather than a hand press. Gág was satisfied with the outcome even if the printing press could not measure up to hand-pulled prints. She concluded, "since it does look good, I don't mind so much having been a prisoner and a slave all these months" (Gág to Scott, 22 March 1941, CLRC). In late July, Dobbs requested three or four drawings for the forthcoming Coward-McCann fall catalog. Gág also designed a promotion poster with an overlay to show the dog's increasing visibility.

The contract sent to Gág in September 1941 guaranteed her 10 percent royalties on the first 7,500 copies, 12.5 percent on copies 7,500 to 12,500, and 15 percent thereafter. The book was officially published 22 September. In October, Gág wrote to a fan, "I've just delivered myself of another book—Nothing At All" (Gág to Kirkman, 22 October 1941, CLRC). The thirty-two page book sold for $1.50.

Special friends and reviewers received advance copies. Dobbs wrote to Gág that she had become "'busy getting dizzy' while re-reading the book to young children" (Dobbs to Gág, 27 August 1941, CLRC). Following the book's publication, the usual reviewers made their predictably favorable comments. Warren Chappell, Alice M. Jordan, and L. G. Kerr all reviewed *Nothing at All* for *Horn Book;* therefore, Anne Carroll Moore, who usually reviewed for that magazine, submitted her appraisal to *Commonweal.* Becker, who usually wrote for the *New York Herald Tribune,* contributed her evaluation to the American Library Association's *Booklist.* Eaton, in the *New York Times,* suggested that the book was "perhaps even more lovable" than *Millions of Cats.*[7] In contrast, an unidentified reviewer for the British *Junior Bookshelf* commented that the book showed "lively and original imagination," but concluded negatively on the Faber and Faber edition published the next year in 1942.[8] The reviewer mistakenly observed that the pictures were smaller than those in *Millions of Cats* and concluded, "I cannot feel that the book is up to the high standard reached by most of this author's earlier work."

Nothing at All lacks the vitality of *Millions of Cats*. The narrative describes rather than reveals action, such as in the sentence, "When Pointy and Curly heard this, they knew they would be safe and happy, so they snuggled into the children's arms and went back to sleep" (*Nothing*). Dialogue might have enhanced the text as a substitute for "Nothing-at-all was wide awake and ready to try his magic" (*Nothing*). Some text could have been deleted to prevent redundancy, for example, "Do you think he was a dog whom anyone could see? No, he wasn't" (*Nothing*). Furthermore, a jackdaw is a peculiar choice for a creature who teaches magic, for the bird lacks any traditional association with enchantment. Even the words "nothingy" and "somethingy" seem contrived. Nevertheless, Gág's reputation as a storyteller and artist made the book a success. She did succeed in drawing an invisible dog and, moreover, a whirling invisible dog.

The Caldecott and Newbery Awards eluded Gág once again, as Robert McCloskey won the former for *Make Way for Ducklings* and Walter Edmonds won the latter for *The Matchlock Gun*, both new on the award list.[9] *Nothing at All* was among the four Caldecott Honor Books named for 1942. Nevertheless, as early as October 1941 the need for reprinting the picture book became obvious. Eight thousand of the 12,500 copies printed had sold immediately, prompting the scheduling of another 10,000 for the second printing. Because of the war, new government rules on limiting paper usage reduced the printing to 5,000 copies. Correcting proofs for the reprints of her other books placed an added demand on Gág's time, but she insisted that only she could perform the task. Some other commitments suffered.

She neglected both her correspondence and her diary. Gág delayed for five years at least one response to a fan letter about *Growing Pains* (Gág to Hilda Growald, 14 November 1945, CLRC). Not only were the diary entries sporadic during the last ten years of her life, but for several years they were nonexistent. From 1935 to 1938 and from February 1939 to March 1942, her journal keeping collapsed completely. Instead, she kept a separate "day book" to record events chronologically. In the late 1930s, she had admitted to herself that she just didn't write in her diary anymore. "Most of the time I just had no urge for that method of self-expression, and I have no intention of filling up this gap with a chronological resume of events" (Diary, 14 March 1938). On occasion, however, she would sit down to describe even several years at a time and recall the significant events in detail.

The continuing war on the European and Pacific fronts affected Gág both psychologically and practically. She drafted a letter to a Minneapolis

friend in March 1942, "I, like so many others, have found it difficult to
organize myself into a creative human being since Pearl Harbor and all
that has come after it. I have not been able to draw at all—it seemed too
futile and selfish when I knew that so many human beings were being
starved, imprisoned, tortured, mutilated, blown to bits" (Gág to Johan
Egilsrud, 10 March 1942, CLRC).

For the second time in her life, America was at war with Germany, a
situation more difficult for her because of her German heritage. "When I
think of the Germans in New Ulm, I sometimes wonder how those in
Europe could have let themselves get into such a mess . . . the only sign
of anything military that I ever noticed was their childlike interest in
having an old cannon in their parades. But perhaps it was this naive trait
which made it possible for the Germans in Europe to allow themselves
to be so misled" (Gág to Growald, 14 November 1945, CLRC). Both
Humphreys and Howard Gag were involved in defense jobs that took
them away from All Creation.

Three Gay Tales from Grimm

Looking younger than her age, Gág turned fifty on 11 March 1943. This
particular year was to mark a significant change in her personal life. She now
had lived two years longer than each of her parents, and she had gained
recognition as an artist, which was her goal and her father's hope for her.

As Gág had predicted, 1942 brought forth no book, but she had
worked steadily on new ideas for book projects. Twenty years earlier she
had produced preschool materials as a Happiwork Company artist, but
the business collapsed before most of them were in production. Near the
end of 1942, Gág wrote to her editor about the concept of a "Baby's
Library" or "Baby's Bookshelf," suggesting a set of books for children
three years old and younger. Dobbs thwarted both proposals. Close on
the heels of those concepts was a completed manuscript for a juvenile
mystery serial she submitted to her editor in January 1943. Two years
before she had felt "practically tyrannized" if she neglected working on
the mystery.

Dobbs also responded negatively to a draft of the mystery called "The
Fairy Quints," judging the beginning and conclusion to be good, but the
story weak. She even set it aside for a few days, then reread it and arrived
at the same conclusion. In her critique, Dobbs complimented Gág on
the characters, who were lively, and the "little home-like activities"
(Dobbs to Gág, 28 January 1943, CLRC), which should appeal to chil-

dren. She said there were three specific problems—too few events sustaining the plot, too many parallels with the Dionne quintuplets (born 1934 in Ontario, Canada), and too much baby talk. As examples of the latter, she quoted "Poppli," "daddums," "hubbydad," and "muffin-pets." By mid-February, Dobbs concluded that both the "Baby's Bookshelf" and "The Quint Mystery" needed significant development. She proposed instead another Grimm fairy tale, "The Three Feathers," for which a translation draft and rough sketches already existed.

After the publication of *Snow White and the Seven Dwarfs* in 1938, Dobbs had urged Gág to work toward developing another Grimm tale. When Gág's niece, Barbara Jean, was born in the fall of 1939, Dobbs suggested that the event called for "another volume of Grimm" (Dobbs to Gág, 8 November 1939, CLRC). In 1940 and again in early 1942, she coaxed, "How about letting that Grimm tale see the light of day?" (Dobbs to Gág, 13 January 1942, CLRC). After her final plea in October—"I shall need desperately on the fall 1943 list a best seller. On the children's list . . . that means a book by you" (Dobbs to Gág, 25 October 1942, CLRC)—Gág rallied to the challenge.

To "The Three Feathers," Gág added two other Grimm tales that reflect Gág's appreciation of the absurd—"The Clever Wife" and "Goose Hans." These two stories, placed first and last in the book, were "noodle-head" stories, about seemingly stupid individuals. In the first tale, the wife, Kotti, reveals her ignorance in following directions from her patient husband. She places a roast in the vegetable patch to cook, mistaking cabbage-like "cole" for heating "coal." Gág clarified for the reader this play on words. Her husband, Friedel, tells her, "You should have put the meat among the coal in the fireplace, not among the cole plants in the garden" (*Three Tales,* 12). After each episode, Kotti's excuse is "You should have told me." But in contrast to the situation in *Gone Is Gone,* the foolish person triumphs in spite of herself; Kotti's good-natured husband tolerates her follies.

The second tale's title changed from "Simple Sepp" to "The Three Feathers" and was somewhat similar to "The Frog Prince" in Gág's *Tales from Grimm.* Unlike the more familiar fairy tale, it is the prince who lifts up a "Wrinkly Crinkly" toad, which is transformed into a fair maiden. Moreover, the woman rather than the man must perform a daring deed. She leaps through a hoop suspended from the ceiling without hurting herself. The story concludes with the former toad as queen, and Seppli, "who had always been considered so dull and simple, became a good King who reigned wisely and well all his days" (*Three Tales,* 48).

In "Goose Hans" a young man asks his mother for advice in winning the hand of Gretel. He then follows her directives, but one step too late. When his mother tells him to stick a needle in his sleeve, he places the next present—a knife—in his sleeve. Gág omits the first-person pronoun when Hans speaks, making him seem even more stupid. "Will do it next time . . . Will do just as you say, mother" (*Three Tales,* 56), he reiterates after each folly. He ultimately covers himself with honey and then feathers, and sits on a goose's nest to hatch a clutch of eggs. The object of his affection runs home; never would she marry such a stupid person. Gág polished the translations for these stories and reworked the introduction to "The Clever Wife," which Dobbs thought was too similar to *Gone Is Gone.*

Despite Gág's intent to make the illustrations humorous, in part to offset the gloom of the war, they lacked the inspiration and verve of her earlier editions of the Brothers Grimm. She completed sixty-seven preliminary illustrations and then pasted them in a dummy book. After evaluating the placements, Gág drew the final illustrations in a competent, but perfunctory, manner. She conveyed more situational humor, with appropriate costumes and stances for the characters. Kotti carries the door on her back, rotund milkmaids dive through a hoop, and Goose Hans sits on the nest, as the text describes. Cognizant of the child reader, Gág drew six separate cheeses to accompany the text describing Kotti rolling cheeses down the hill. She portrayed Goose Hans as stupid by placing his finger in his mouth and having his feet point inward.

By June the text was in the galley stage, and the illustrations were with the engravers. As usual, Gág insisted that she examine the proofs, providing the quality control for which she was known. To a fan, she wrote in August, "I've been busy all year delivering myself of three more tales from Grimm" (Gág to Leona Henning, 9 August 1943, CLRC). Gág dedicated the book to her nephew, Gary. After much discussion between Gág and Dobbs, *Three Gay Tales from Grimm* was chosen for the title. "The Three Feathers" and "The Clever Wife" were earlier suggestions, and even the preliminary jacket text used the latter.

Coward-McCann published the book in October 1943 in a size and format similar to her *Snow White and the Seven Dwarfs,* published five years earlier. The jacket identifies Gág as "author of *Millions of Cats* [and] *Tales from Grimm.*" Unlike the covers for her earlier books, this one has a collage of illustrations from the interior. While the jacket copy suggests that the fairy tales "will be sure to provide laughter for young and old in a black year of war," the illustrations seem heavy and dull.

Three Gay Tales from Grimm, a sixty-three page book that sold for $1.50, was not a great success. Despite the turning of the tide on the war fronts in favor of the Allies, the public was distracted. Publishers had limited access to publishing materials because of the war, and the binding and paper for Gág's book suffered. Incorporated into the copyright entry was the war regulations clause, "Produced in full compliance with the Government's regulations for conserving paper and other essential materials" (*Three Tales,* iv). While the government assured the publishing industry that the paper deficiency would reverse itself, it did not do so soon enough to benefit Gág's book.

Reviewers paid attention to the book, most of them commenting on the selection of little-known Grimm tales. Predictably, the usual reviewers welcomed the book. Alice M. Jordan, an associate editor of the *Horn Book,* and Eaton reviewed *Three Gay Tales* for the *Horn Book* and the *New York Times,* respectively. Becker mistakenly identified the ink drawings as "jolly woodcuts."[10] Mary Gould Davis, now the New York Public Library storytelling specialist, lauded the book as appropriate for Gág, but criticized the poor binding and printing.[11] An appraisal in the *New Yorker* was less enthusiastic, commenting that the pictures were "not Miss Gág's best."[12] The German-American artist Fritz Eichenberg suggested in the *Horn Book* that it "might not be a bad idea for her to try a new technique that would create renewed interest in her fine work."[13] He commented that *The ABC Bunny* had been a welcome departure from her earlier style, and he expected that she would continue to extend herself.

Gág's selection for *Three Gay Tales from Grimm* seems based more on the fact that she had already translated the tales than that the three had much in common. They are not as humorous as some that would be forthcoming in her next book, such as "The Tailor Who Went to Heaven." While the protagonists in two tales are peasants, a prince is the main character in the middle one. The peasants Kotti and Goose Hans remain foolish, but the prince in "The Three Feathers" proves that he really is wise. Gág's usual sense of humor is limited to a few drawings. She spares the reader a graphic description of the "yellow chips in the barn" (*Three Tales,* 14). Illustrations of Kotti pouring vinegar on the unwary thieves (*Three Tales,* 25) and Simple Sepp's scrawny and fat brothers (37) are closer to slapstick humor. They do, however, demonstrate her capable craftsmanship in designing for the whole page or only a portion.

Despite the occasional remarkable illustration, most reviewers and award committees remained unenthusiastic about *Three Gay Tales from Grimm.* The Caldecott Award for books published in 1943, which eluded Gág once again, went to Louis Slobodkin for his distinguished illustrations for James Thurber's *Many Moons.* Esther Forbes won the Newbery Award for the distinguished writing of *Johnny Tremain,* illustrated by Lynd

Ward.[14] *Three Gay Tales from Grimm* failed even to be selected among the Honor Books for either award. While a Canadian publisher, Longmans, Green, in Toronto, issued *Three Gay Tales from Grimm* the same day as did Coward-McCann, other international publishers seemed reluctant to publish the book. Faber and Faber of Great Britain, which had published her earlier books, declined to take this one. Another British company, William Heinemann, published it three years later in 1946. The book was produced shabbily even after the war ended. Great Britain, too, used poor materials. A statement similar to that required in the American book notes that the volume was "produced in complete conformity with the authorized economy standards." Unfortunately, the cover, designed with white vignettes superimposed on a red background, was even less effective than the American version, and the number "3" substituted for the word "three." An anonymous reviewer in *Junior Bookshelf* was enthusiastic about the translation but less so about the drawings. "Wanda Gág is undoubtedly the best translator we have because she has been so completely saturated in the spirit of the Household Tales. Yet, do I detect a falling off, a rather more sophisticated attitude in this new collection of stories?" The same reviewer considered the illustrations a "little stylized," showing "too much evidence of the artist's sense of design."[15]

Nevertheless, the book pleased some individuals and libraries. The Minneapolis Public Library requested permission to reproduce the illustration of Kotti in "The Clever Wife" pouring vinegar on thieves. A full-color mural remains in the children's library storytelling room to this day.

Marriage and More Projects

The year 1943 was one of departure from certain principles for Gág. Thomas Coward challenged Gág's policy about illustrating only her own work. He wrote a confidential letter to her, asking if she would illustrate a fairy tale rewritten by Rose Dobbs. In this case, Gág remained true to form and responded negatively, reiterating her policy that she would illustrate only her own books. Fritz Eichenberg illustrated Dobbs's book, *No Room, an Old Story,* published the next year by Coward-McCann. But Gág did complete a drawing for an adult poetry book written by her Minnesota friend Johan Egilsrud. Perhaps she felt an obligation to him, as her siblings had stayed in his family's home briefly while waiting to move into their first Minneapolis apartment. Gág saw him occasionally when he visited New York City, and they corresponded during the intervening years. Having received a doctoral degree in comparative literature in 1934 from the Sorbonne in Paris, Egilsrud now taught in the English department at the University of Minnesota. He requested a drawing for the frontispiece opposite the title page, but instead used Adolf Dehn's drawing there and placed Gág's in the interior. Five hundred copies of the book, *Pond Image,* sold out in ten days, but it was not reprinted.[16]

Gág's other departure from long-standing principle came in the form of her marriage to Earle Marshall Humphreys on 27 August 1943. As mentioned in chapter 1, the couple feared Humphreys might be fired from his job for lax morals because they lived together without being married (Diary, 23 August 1943). On those grounds, Gág agreed that they should marry. They intended to be married in Poughkeepsie to ensure their privacy and completed their blood tests there, but the ceremony took place at Central Baptist Church on 92d Street and Amsterdam Avenue in New York City, with Gág's brother-in-law Robert Janssen as a witness.

The clergyman promised there would be no publicity, but apparently he did not recognize Gág's name anyway. Gág wore a white and blue plaid seersucker summer suit, silk stockings, and a new hairstyle; Humphreys wore a gray serge suit with no vest. Following the ceremony, Humphreys had to report to work, and Gág returned to their apartment in New York City.

Gág was surprisingly satisfied with her new marital status. "But I must admit that, altho we laughed over it and didn't take it too seriously, and altho we had agreed that we would give each other the same freedom as we had before, we do feel *different* and more married, and paradoxically more *full* . . . it made me feel more at ease with this world of law and 'morality' in which we were obliged to move . . . if two people have held each other's trust and interest for twenty years without legal bonds a much deeper stronger bond has already been forged." She added, however, that their previous relationship, "without benefit of clergy and marriage bureau, was a true and moral one" (Diary, 23 August 1943).

For some years, at least since 1934, Gág worked on several drafts that she called her "Childhood Reminiscences." She perceived them as being different from a biography, more "interpretive and philosophical," covering the years prior to her diary writing (Gág to Scott, 26 November 1943, MHS). While working on them she realized her "sentence structure needed improvement" (Gág to Scott, 11 October 1944, MHS), which reading a book about writing techniques helped solve. Five reminiscences were transcribed from her handwriting to typescript. "Wanda and God" consists of observations about religion from the point of view of a child raised in the home of a "free-thinker." "Going to the Butcher

Shop" depicts Gág's reaction to her mother having another child and to being teased when her middle name (Hazel) is misunderstood as "Esel" (German for "donkey"). "Going Down to Grandma's" recalls Gág's following the railroad tracks to her grandmother's country home, where there were gardens and food and kittens. "Paper Dolls" describes the Gág children making paper dolls from Sears Roebuck catalogue models and surrounding them with handmade furniture.[17] "Snowshoveling" reveals Gág's naive reaction to literature, such as the confusion of Cupid shooting an arrow into a poet's heart.[18] Left handwritten were three more, "Grab Bag," "Playing Dentist," and "Sandstone."[19]

Look magazine invited Gág, along with six other artists, to submit an original illustration for a Christmas issue. Appearing in the same collage were Disney characters, James Daugherty's Andy peering at the lion, Kurt Wiese's Freddie and Ping, Hardie Gramatky's "Little Toot," and Gustaf Tenggren's "The Little Match Girl." Gág contributed the little old man and woman with the kitten from Millions of Cats for the centerfold with the caption, "Characters Children Love."[20]

Life continued as usual. During this time Gág frequently resurrected projects from previous decades. She revised scripts she had written for Millions of Cats and Nothing at All and read them for radio broadcast. She submitted a drawing for the Children's Book Week slogan, "Build the Future with Books," but the committee selected another piece for the annual poster. A staff person from Lippincott asked Gág to illustrate an edition of Grimm, but Gág concluded that it would conflict with sales of her own book.

Dobbs proposed a nativity book for all ages, using the Bible text. Humphreys, raised as a Baptist and despite his embrace of atheism, had urged her to illustrate the Bible since 1928. Although Gág did not profess Christianity, she nevertheless found the topic of the birth of Jesus interesting. In the early 1930s she had discussed illustrating a book of Bible stories with Humphreys (Diary, 13 April 1932). By mid-October, Gág expressed a desire to prepare a humorous version of the birth of Jesus. She envisioned it as similar to her drawing "Nativity," which appeared in the 20 December 1936 Christmas issue of the New York Herald Tribune book section almost a decade earlier. Nothing ever came of this project.

While another book did not materialize in 1944 or 1945, Gág's work became more familiar to the American public. A traveling exhibit sponsored by the American Association of University Women (AAUW) opened in September 1944. Entitled "Wanda Gág Prints & Books," the exhibit included a range of work from an etching made in 1927, "Vase with Flowers," to a linoleum cut from 1943, "Self Portrait." Thirty-three pieces of art and ten books were listed on the printed flyer, accompanied by a reproduction of "Lamplight" from 1929.

Gág agreed with the intent of the organization to send traveling exhibits to cities that had a population of less than 50,000 and no museum. Her hometown was an example of such a place. The organization matted and insured the selections and arranged for the tour. Profits from sales would go to the artist (Gág to Newton, 17 May 1944, CLRC). The exhibit's first site was the Alabama Polytechnic Institute. The AAUW selected other sites primarily in the Midwest, such as Bismarck, North Dakota; Green Bay, Wisconsin; and Franklin, Indiana. At the conclusion of twenty-three showings over two years, more than 15,000 individuals had viewed Gág's work (Lura Beam to Dobbs, 9 September 1946, CLRC).

A lithograph done on stone entitled "Whodunit" (1944) was her spoof on both her fairy-tale books and her prints, as some critics had perceived a dark side to her personality. Paper cut-outs similar to the gingerbread cookie figures in the introduction of "Hansel and Gretel" in *Tales from Grimm* march into the print from the left side; tenpins line up to the right. Boots that may have been worn by the wicked stepmother in *Snow White and the Seven Dwarfs* stand empty. The barefoot legs of a man covered with straw emerge from the barn, and there is evidence of footprints on sawed logs. A hand reaches up from the barn to grab a lantern, the only source of light. Although Gág worked on the stone, she did not make any prints for the public during her lifetime. Prints were made the year after her death.

More Tales from Grimm

Gág began her plan to translate and illustrate the Brothers Grimm fairy tales in the late 1920s. She originally intended to translate sixty stories from German to English and illustrate them "profusely" for a three-volume set. The first volume from a decade earlier, *Tales from Grimm,* contained sixteen tales. For the most part, they were familiar, long, and appealing to children. Four others were translated and illustrated by Gág and appeared in *Snow White and the Seven Dwarfs* and *Three Gay Tales from Grimm.*

Further development of the project had to be delayed. "I have many good intentions, but Life insists on having some say in one's plans," she wrote to Edith Newton. Gág thought she had "recurring intestinal flu" (Gág to Newton, 17 May 1944, CLRC). Gág finally admitted that she was seriously ill early in 1945. She entered a hospital in February and agreed to exploratory surgery in March. Some close friends knew she was hospitalized, but lacked information about the seriousness of her condition, which was diagnosed as cancer. Her publisher Thomas Coward wrote to Humphreys, "We all have a special feeling about Wanda here . . . her delightful personality and her loyalty endeared her to all of us" (Coward to Humphreys, 19 March 1945, CLRC). Meanwhile, World War II was ending; the Germans surrendered on 8 May 1945, the Japanese on 2 September.

Gág abandoned her manuscript, "The Mystery of the Quintuplets," because Dobbs considered it too sentimental. As usual, Gág declined an invitation from another children's book editor, Helen Dean Fish, now at Lippincott. She asked this time if Gág would illustrate an edition of the Brothers Grimm, envisioned as part of a classics series designed by Helen Gentry (Fish to Gág, 23 July 1945, CLRC). Instead she renewed her efforts on another volume of Grimm, tentatively titled "Treasures from Grimm." Even before she became ill she preferred writing while in bed; she now used the couch at All Creation. Working on fairy tales soothed Gág's spirits while she was ill. Gág read the tales in German, selected thirty-five to translate, and compared her drafts with some translated by others and already published. She regarded herself as the one who could capture the spirit of the text and again used the expression "freely translated."

Gág's choice of tales from approximately two hundred written by the Brothers Grimm reveals much about her own personality. She couldn't resist retelling tales about cats. In "The Cat and the Fox," the arrogant fox who brags that he is "master of a hundred arts and wiles" succumbs to the hunting dogs, while the cat survives with only the ability to climb (*More Tales*, 62). A cat is brought to the palace to rid it of mice in "The Three Lucky Ones." Gág conveys its increasingly desperate voice as "Maiu!" and then "May-ow" (*More Tales*, 194–95), giving it unusual character and personality. As she did for *Tales from Grimm*, Gág added a cat in illustrations for "The Sorcerer's Apprentice."

She preferred the shorter, sophisticated, and subtle tales for her third collected volume. Four of the fairy tales—"Lucky Scraps," "The Cat and the Fox," "A Trip to Schlaffenland," and "Star Dollar"—were anecdotes. She included "Lucky Scraps," which tells of a young man who, when he discovers that his intended bride was lazy and wasteful, chooses to marry her enterprising maid instead. This suited Gág's work ethic, introduced in her youth by her father. In "Star Dollar," an orphan girl gives her scrap of bread to an old man and then her cap, jacket, dress, and even undergarments to children even more poor. She shivers in the dark only momentarily, for from the heavens falls a linen dress and stars that become silver dollars. Gág had experienced hunger and the lack of stylish clothes as a teenager, and this story suited her sense of justice.

Gág deliberately eliminated some tales involving religion that she had translated and tentatively considered. She also ignored tales referring to the Virgin Mary, an important figure in the Roman Catholic religion ascribed to by many in her hometown, New Ulm. She included two tales, "The Three Languages" and "The Tailor Who Went to Heaven," that make slightly sarcastic or light-hearted references to religious beliefs. After a pope dies, cardinals in Rome anoint a seemingly stupid boy in "The Three Languages." Doves sitting on his shoulders coach him to sing the Latin Mass. In "The Tailor Who Went to Heaven," a tailor flings a golden stool down to earth when he observes a theft.

Gág eventually deleted "Flower Riddle," "Golden Sleigh," and "Knoist and His Sons." Later, following Gág's death, Dobbs dropped "The Idol." In each of two tales, "The Seven Swabians" and "The Wolf and the Seven Little Kids," there were seven siblings, reminiscent of the seven Gag children. Mother Nanny's affection for her children shines through the text as Lissi's love had touched the Gags. "And so, with the wicked wolf out of the way, they and their mother lived happily ever after" (*More Tales,* 249).

Gág struggled to arrive at an accurate translation of the titles and names of characters and places, as well as German idioms. Her notes indicate that she referred to other English translations, such as those by Lucy Crane and Mrs. Edgar Lucas. On her own manuscripts she jotted down the page numbers from other translations for reference. On her draft of "The Wolf and the Seven Kids," she penciled in page references from six other versions for reference, such as "Lucas" and "Kredel" (Gág, manuscript for *More Tales from Grimm,* CLRC). She probably used the Fritz Kredel edition for the translation of nuances and idiom. A native-born German, Kredel both translated and illustrated with woodcuts his *Grimm's Fairy Tales,* published by Stackpole in 1937.[21]

Gág took more liberties in her translation. She changed tentative titles from "Dull Hanse" to "The Earthly Gnome," "Father's Legacy" to "The Three Lucky Ones," and "The Magician's Apprentice" to "The Sorcerer's Apprentice." Names of the sons in "The Seven Swabians" changed under her close scrutiny, but she retained "Hickelty Hunkipuss" for the maid. She also retained place names such as "Buxtehude Heath" and "Schlaraffenland." Gág dealt with change of voice. For example, the narrator in the text interacts with the reader in a passage in "Earth Gnome": "I am sure you can guess the rest" (*More Tales,* 186). "Iron Hans" concludes with, "I will leave you to guess whether this was a happy wedding festival or not" (*More Tales,* 228).

After drafting the translations, Gág began work on the illustrations. She referred to working on preliminary drawings as "problem solving." First, Gág sketched tentative lines on the holograph manuscript. The next step was drawing in pencil, and she completed some 132 preliminary sketches on tracing paper. Finally, she outlined with India ink. One illustration—for "Star Dollar"—appeared in color and served for both the cover and the frontispiece illustration for *More Tales from Grimm.*

With all the drawings, Gág enhanced and interpreted the text carefully for children. Some illustrators of earlier editions of "The Shoemaker and the Elves" portrayed fully clothed elves, which contradicts the sense of the story. Gág, on the other hand, purposefully drew them naked as they made shoes on the workbench. At the conclusion of the fairy tale, they put on the clothing newly made for them by the shoemaker and his wife. Illustrations clarify unfamiliar words such as "scullery boy" and "cudgel" in "Table, Donkey, and Cudgel-in-the-Sack." The pin in the innkeeper's hand towel and the needle in the cushion appear in the pictures accompanying "The Good-for-Nothings" (*More Tales,* 81). In "The Tailor Who Went to Heaven," wings on the golden armchair used by God suggest a heavenly setting. A sign outside the Sorcerer's shop identifies its purpose: "Good charms worked here" (*More Tales,* 205).

In contrast to her unique earlier fairy-tale interpretations, Gág was more redundant in her choice of art. Several illustrations in the posthumously published book repeat images from her earlier books. A row of neatly made beds in "The Six Swans" resembles those of the seven dwarfs. The shimmering apple in "Iron Hans" (*More Tales,* 223) almost duplicates the first illustration in *The ABC Bunny.* Because she worked methodically, a sufficient number of illustrations existed in final or rough state to support a book, even though she died before it was completed. In the foreword, Zigrosser begins "This is Wanda Gág's last book" (*More Tales,* v). He then explains that some of the illustrations remained in a preliminary state because of Gág's premature death, but he hastens to add that this gave the reader a chance to view a "work in progress."

Humphreys assisted Dobbs by gathering both the completed and the tentative illustrations together, and Coward-McCann published *More Tales from Grimm* in 1947, the year after Gág died. The company substituted the title for Gág's working title, "Treasures from Grimm." The volume contains thirty-two fairy tales, twice the number of the first volume, *Tales from Grimm.* Eleven children on the dedication page are identified by their given names, including Gág's niece and Alma Scott's daughters.

While the year 1945 brought peace to the world in the aftermath of World War II, it forebode terminal illness for Gág. Grolier postponed the contract deadline for her illustrations for an "East of the Sun and West of the Moon" story to be included in *The Book of Knowledge.*[22] She worked on ink drawings. Two were snow scenes. In one, the White Bear forges through sharp-edged ice and heavy snowflakes with a serene princess astride, and in the other an old woman sits holding a golden apple in an icy cave entrance. Along with this project, Dobbs urged Gág to consider a spring 1946 deadline for the next volume of the Grimm fairy tales.

After an operation, Gág returned to All Creation in June 1945. She lay on a couch with notebook in hand, alternating between translating the Grimm fairy tales and writing her childhood reminiscences. At Christmastime, Humphreys and Gág left for Florida, where they kept up their routine activities and tried to retain their privacy. Despite her lack of energy, she polished the translations of thirty-three fairy tales for the next Grimm book, and Humphreys typed them. When they visited the Hollywood Library, they informed the librarian that Gág was engaged in comparing illustrations in fine contemporary books with those she read as a child. Gág then checked the engraver's proof for the eight "East of the Sun" illustrations and mailed them to New York City. She also saved the company from embarrassment. The proof mistakenly credited the Danish-American artist Kay Nielsen as the author of the Norwegian tale collected by Peter Christen Asbjornsen and Jorgen Moe. Grolier published the volume in 1947. In addition to using her newly created illustrations for this story, Grolier reproduced several from *Tales from Grimm* and *More Tales from Grimm* for its encyclopedia.

When Coward-McCann published the 272-page *More Tales from Grimm* in fall 1947, it sold for a mere $2.75. Reviewers lamented Gág's passing. In her review for the *New York Times,* Ellen Lewis Buell perceived "no hint" of Gág's illness permeating the book, but rather "gaiety and cunning skill."[23] Moreover, she concluded that the reader gained insight into a work in progress.

Reviewers Moore and Becker looked back on Gág's eighteen-year career as a children's book author, illustrator, and translator. They reviewed both her debut, *Millions of Cats,* and her last book. Moore praised Gág's "high spirit in the rendering of the stories,"[24] and Becker added a eulogy: "There is a sure way to go on living on this earth, not as a memory but as a presence. It is to make a book that children take to their hearts and pass on to other children. Wanda Gág made many such: this is the last."[25] Gág's original intent fifteen years earlier had been to illustrate about sixty Grimm fairy tales; she completed fifty-one.

Gág's last book, *More Tales from Grimm,* became a companion piece to *Tales from Grimm,* published eleven years earlier. Even if Gág had completed all the final illustrations she planned, the book could not have made an impact similar to the first. The mood of the country was different. America emerged victorious from the war and people looked excitedly at technological innovations. Television eroded reading time for families. German fairy tales hardly took front stage. For the most part, the tales in the companion volume are less familiar, and the best known—"The Sorcerer's Apprentice," "The Wolf and the Seven Little Kids," and "The Shoemaker and the Elves"—are among the last four fairy tales in the book.

Gág's book was not even a close contender for the American Library Association awards. The Newbery Award for books published in 1947 went to William Pène du Bois for *The Twenty-One Balloons,* and the Caldecott Award went to Roger Duvoisin for *White Snow Bright Snow.*[26] But Wanda Gág did receive the ample recognition she sought as an artist. Exhibits throughout the country and national newspaper coverage confirmed her fame. By 1940 her art was on exhibit somewhere in the country almost every week and her books were in libraries and bookstores. Even two years before her death, Gág conveyed to her biographer, "I *did* carry out his [Papa's] wish of finishing what he was obliged to leave undone. . . . I do not face life saying 'I have done this,' but 'Papa and I have done this'" (Gág to Scott, 16 January 1944, MHS).

Chapter Six
Cinderella Worked Hard: Aftermath

In a unique way, Wanda Gág succeeded in her dual career as a fine art printmaker and as an author and illustrator of children's books. She was an important figure in the development of American children's books from both a historical and a contemporary perspective. Gág set a high standard from her debut in 1928 with the innovative and spirited *Millions of Cats* through her translations of Grimm in the mid-1940s. She was personally satisfied with her contribution to children's literature and enjoyed her fame. Her reputation continued to be held in high esteem even on the centenary year of her birth, 1993.

Historical Context, 1928–1946

Gág affected trends in both text and illustration in her lifetime. Her own stories differed from one another in plot, characters, and setting but possessed the same fairy-tale-like construction. Public acceptance of fairy tales themselves ebbed and flowed during the decades in which she worked. For example, during an era in the 1930s when some believed these tales damaged the psyche and were therefore inappropriate for children, Gág translated and illustrated a selection by the Brothers Grimm. She championed fairy tales in a lecture in November 1938 at the New York Public Library (which was published as "I Like Fairy Tales" in the *Horn Book* the following year). Forty years later, in *The Uses of Enchantment: The Meaning and Importance of Fairy Tales,*[1] child psychiatrist Bruno Bettelheim reassured parents and professionals that fairy tales assisted children in their coping with reality.

Gág had already achieved a reputation in the fine arts when she turned to children's books. She reverted to the nineteenth-century black-ink medium used for newspaper and magazine illustration. Gág continued to use it effectively, despite a developing trend among other illustrators toward bright, flat color. Her books proved that black and white remained as effective as the use of more costly multicolor pictures by illustrators such

as Maud and Miska Petersham. Gág also revived hand-lettered text. After
her success, some subsequent book artists used the concepts she had rein-
troduced. Her innovation was designing together the text and art, using to
full advantage the two pages of the opened book, the double-page spread.
The most reputable reviewers in the graphic arts and children's book
arenas commended her on these achievements. Gág's shows at the Weyhe
Gallery in New York City in 1926 and 1928 launched her reputation as a
printmaker. She was included in *Who's Who in American Art,*[2] *Who's Who
in America,*[3] the *American Art Annual,*[4] and *Mallet's Index of Artists.*[5]

Anne Carroll Moore's reviews spanned Gág's productive lifetime, covering both her 1928 debut in children's literature and her last work,
published in 1947. As the New York Public Library's head of children's
work, she used her influence to promote Gág as a notable author-illustrator. Storytellers and librarians throughout the New York City library
system used Gág's books. Historical records indicate that *Millions of Cats*
was read aloud frequently in the main library and branches. An advertisement in a New York City newspaper announced storyteller Mary
Gould Davis's reading of *Gone Is Gone* at a library branch shortly after
the work was published. And Moore had literally demanded that Gág
produce a *Snow White and the Seven Dwarfs* to offset what she believed to
be the distortions of the story in the Disney movie and the plethora of
ensuing Disney books.

In addition to Moore, artist Lynd Ward always appraised Gág's books
in a favorable light. Because Ward's novel in woodcuts, *God's Man,*
sealed his reputation in 1929, his accolades made an impact on the reading public. He reviewed her second book, *Snippy and Snappy,* and out-
lived her to write an essay in the *Horn Book* memorial issue about Gág.
Artist Rockwell Kent was another admirer.

Reviewers typically compared Gág's later books with her debut,
Millions of Cats. Anne T. Eaton, for example, stated that *Snippy and
Snappy* was less universal than *Millions of Cats*[6]; and Rachel Field noted
that the book was "in the mood of her popular *Millions of Cats*" (Field
1931, 296). A reviewer for the British journal *Junior Bookshelf* remarked
about *Nothing at All,* "I had hoped, though it didn't seem possible, that
Wanda Gág's new book might be as good as her masterpiece, *Millions of
Cats.* Well, it isn't. But who cares?" ("New Books," 95). Englishman
Marcus S. Crouch stated that "*Millions of Cats* . . . was the first and is still
the best of her original work" (Crouch, 51).

Ruth Sawyer, in *The Way of the Storyteller,* urged parents to share picture books with their children to establish the reading habit. She com-

mented that *Millions of Cats* has never failed to reach eager young hands and imaginations. Moreover, she noted that *Gone Is Gone* has "become a dearly loved classic for all ages."[7]

While reviewers recommended these books, Gág's publisher promoted them and bookstores sold them. New York City doubled as both the publishing center for children's books and the hub of bookstores, concentrated primarily in a triangle with Boston and Philadelphia. Cleveland and Chicago were also good bookselling cities, while Minneapolis and St. Paul were somewhat on the periphery. At some time in her career, Gág autographed her books at prominent book and department stores, such as Lord and Taylor and Macy's, in each of these cities.

None of Wanda Gág's books received the Newbery or Caldecott Awards, despite the eminence of her reviewers and the enthusiasm of the public. The medals bring the most prestigious American honor to children's book writing and illustrating, respectively. Two picture books, *Millions of Cats* and *The ABC Bunny,* were Newbery Honor Books (formerly termed Runners-Up), and two others, *Snow White and the Seven Dwarfs* and *Nothing at All,* were Caldecott Honor Books. Had the Caldecott Award for distinguished illustration been established by 1929 instead of 1938, her *Millions of Cats* would surely have been the winner. It was the only picture book among the Honor Books of that year for the Newbery Award and, moreover, the only one to remain in print to this day. Despite the lack of the top awards, Gág's books sold well. While other artists suffered financially after the stock market crash and during the Depression, Gág earned a steady income from book royalties and for some years was able to maintain two residences—her country home in New Jersey and a rented room or modest apartment in New York City.

Along with the library association book award committees, the American Institute of Graphic Arts (AIGA) acknowledged Gág's books. In 1952, a five-person jury retrospectively selected *Millions of Cats* and *The ABC Bunny* as among the most outstanding children's books published between 1920 and 1952.[8] They judged entries on typography and artistic merit. The graphic arts judges also chose *More Tales from Grimm* for another AIGA exhibit covering the years 1945 to 1959.

Wanda Gág, both as a creator of art and as a person, intrigued journalists and critics. Elisabeth Luther Cary, author and art critic for the *New York Times* for twenty years, wrote several articles about Gág. She covered exhibitions for the *Times* showcasing Gág's work from 1929 through 1931. Cary interviewed Gág for an article, "Casual Impressions of Modernism," for *American Magazine of Art,*[9] and she appraised Gág's work along with

that of Peggy Bacon in an essay for *Prints*,[10] selecting four Gág graphics
to accompany her insights. Carl Zigrosser wrote articles and a book on
graphic arts in America in which he commented on Gág. He arranged to
reproduce her print "Lamplight" for *Creative Art*[11] and the wood engraving "Spinning Wheel" to accompany his essay a decade later for the
Studio.[12] Zigrosser selected Gág for one of his twenty-four close-ups of
contemporary printmakers in his book, *The Artist in America,* published
in 1942, where she took her place among such notables as Thomas Hart
Benton, Adolf Dehn, and Alfred Stieglitz.[13]

Young people learned about the woman Wanda Gág, too. In 1934,
Winifred and Frances Kirkland selected Gág as the subject for their first
chapter, "Wanda Gág, Who Followed Her Own Way," in their *Girls Who
Became Artists.* Only a year before, the *Classmate: A Paper for Young People,*
had published almost the same text as "She Followed Her Bent," accompanied by a small photograph of Gág and examples of her illustrations.
Both concluded with, "Today she stands unique among artists for her
insight that can see beauty even in sordidness, and for her sure craftsmanship that can reveal that beauty to others."[14] She was also among
the two hundred individuals asked to write an autobiographical sketch
for the reference book, *The Junior Book of Authors.*[15]

By 1940, Gág was listed in Marquis' *Who's Who.* In 1942 she was
included among the 1,850 entries in *Twentieth Century Authors.*[16]
Ironically, Carmen Richards omitted Gág from her *Minnesota Writers.*[17]
When a letter had arrived with Richards's request for an autobiographical essay, Gág was ill and referred the matter to her publisher. Richards
rejected the mimeographed information forwarded by Coward-McCann.

Gág made a direct impact as well on the creation of children's books
by others. In 1930 she encouraged Flavia to illustrate children's books
and to write about what they had done as children (Gág to Flavia Gag,
24 September 1930, Harm). She also advised Flavia that books paid better than magazine stories and that material for twelve to eighteen year
olds was in demand. Flavia then wrote and illustrated *Sing a Song of
Seasons* for Coward-McCann. During and after Wanda Gág's lifetime,
Flavia created more books and illustrated others. One task was illustrating Alma Scott's *The Story of Kattor,* which Gág also critiqued. Surprisingly, Flavia produced picture stories for the Christian children's
magazine market despite her free thinking and nonreligious background.

Evidence in her considerable correspondence suggests that Gág inspired other authors and illustrators of children's books. For instance, Gág
gave information about publishers to Ellis Credle, who created *Down,*

Down the Mountain in 1934 and *Across the Cotton Patch* in 1935 (Gág to Credle, 22 January and 4 May 1938, CLRC).[18] To a striving author from Kansas, Gág recommended a book on composition (Gág to Raye Kirkman, 22 October 1941, CLRC). Indirectly, Gág affected the work of both Virginia Lee Burton, who won the Caldecott Award in 1943 for *The Little House,* and Marie Hall Ets, who received one in 1960 for *Nine Days to Christmas.*[19] Historian Barbara Bader, in her essay "A Second Look: *Millions of Cats,*" surmises that Burton "translated Gág's primitivism and near-pointillist techniques into color."[20] Ets, who created characters such as "Mister Penny" and his farm animals, stated that Wanda Gág was one of her favorite author-illustrators (Ets to the author, 4 August 1963, CLRC). Ets also illustrated in black and white but with a medium she developed called "paper batik."

Responses to Gág's Death, 1946–1947

Obituaries appeared in the national press immediately following Wanda Gág's death in 1946. Bertha E. Mahoney wrote an essay about two artists who had died recently—N. C. Wyeth and Wanda Gág—for the *Horn Book*'s early fall issue.[21] Along with the editor Mahoney, members of the magazine's editorial board—Louise Seaman Bechtel, Anne Carroll Moore, and Alice M. Jordan—had reviewed at least one of Gág's books. In 1947 the *Horn Book* devoted an issue "In tribute to Wanda Gág" to which Gág's professional and personal acquaintances contributed essays. Retired from the New York Public Library since 1941, Moore wrote the introductory editorial entitled "Art for Life's Sake." She quoted from Gág's *Growing Pains* and other writings about the author-illustrator's high regard for children's books.[22] Alma Schmidt Scott, Gág's friend from New Ulm days, provided the biographical sketch, a precursor to her soon-to-be-published biography.[23] Critic Carl Zigrosser appraised Gág as an artist.[24] Gág's first editor, Ernestine Evans, reminisced about Gág's seemingly natural writing skills in the previously mentioned "Wanda Gág as Writer." The *Horn Book* later reprinted Evans's essay in a compilation of articles from the magazine's first twenty-five years.[25] Gág's second editor, Rose Dobbs, contributed "Wanda Gág, Fellow-Worker," describing her illustrations and relationship with printers.[26] Lynd Ward, who would receive the 1953 Caldecott Award for *The Biggest Bear,* wrote the essay, "Wanda Gág, Fellow-Artist."[27] Gág's husband, Earle Humphreys, selected for publication and edited letters from children.[28] Robert Janssen's photographs of his sister-in-law and her surroundings, along with samples of Gág's drawing, were interspersed with the text. The memorial issue concluded with "The Cat and the Fox," one of Gág's translations of the Grimm fairy tales scheduled for publication in the fall of 1947 in *More Tales from Grimm*.[29] Along with the obituaries and the *Horn Book*'s memorial issue, several exhibits celebrated Gág's life. The Minneapolis Institute of Arts held a memorial exhibit, scheduled originally from 10 August to 9 September 1946 and extended to 31 October because of popular demand.[30] In the fall, the Philadelphia Museum of Art—to which the executors of the estate had donated some of her drawings, watercolors, and prints—exhibited part of this acquisition from 16 October to 24 November 1946. Also on display were some of her etching tools and lithograph stones, as well as her children's books. The New York Public Library exhibited Wanda Gág's books in the Central Children's Room from 23 June to 1 November 1947, accompanied by a pamphlet noting Gág's use of the library when she was engaged in research on the fairy tales of the Brothers Grimm. Meanwhile, the American Association of University Women sponsored another traveling show of Gág's work.

Critical Appraisal, 1948–Present

Exhibits of Gág's work continued and her name retained importance in children's literature and art circles. The New Ulm Public Library held two exhibitions of her work twenty years apart, in 1948 and 1968. In the 1978 commemoration of the fiftieth anniversary of the publication of Gág's first children's book, the Graduate School of Library Science at the University of Texas exhibited letters, drawings, and memorabilia from the Harold A. Larrabee Collection of Wanda Gág.[31] Later, a 1980 exhibit entitled "Three Women Artists" at the University of Minnesota's University Gallery featured Gág along with Frances Cranmer Greenman and Clara Mairs.[32] The Art Complex Museum in Duxbury, Massachusetts, exhibited Gág's prints and publications from 5 February to 24 April 1994. In conjunction with the show were programs of puppeteering and storytelling and a display of children's art.

Reference works, books, and journals in children's literature and art history have included reference to Gág in every decade since *Millions of Cats* was published. The University of Minnesota Press published *Wanda Gág: The Story of an Artist* by Alma Scott in 1949 and marketed it to both teenagers and adults. Two-thirds of the book covered Gág's formative years before she produced significant prints and books. The detailed text tends toward subjectivity. Robert Walker provided an extensive review of the biography for the *Horn Book*.[33] Scott later condensed her biography for an entry in *Notable American Women, 1607–1950,* published by the Belknap Press of Harvard University Press.[34] Wanda Gág was among the editors' selection of only twenty-seven children's authors for commentary.

Over the years, other professionals such as educators,[35] librarians, and journalists have written critical biographical sketches intended for children or adults. In 1950, *Trails for Juniors,* a Methodist Board of Education publication for children, published Jane P. Renshaw's "Wanda Wouldn't Stop Drawing."[36] Thirty years later, Minnesotan Mary Ann Nord contributed "Wanda Gág Makes a Wish Come True" for *Roots,* a publication for children from the Minnesota Historical Society.[37] She selected appropriate illustrations different from those in *Growing Pains,* emphasizing Gág's childhood and teenage years

Librarians, too, appreciated Gág's work. Virginia Haviland—the first children's literature specialist at the Library of Congress—upheld *Millions of Cats* as "among the [three] most widely beloved picture books."[38] The title of her essay for the *Library Journal* published in 1961 uses Gág's phrase, "Among the 'Millions and Billions and Trillions' of Books." Children's librarians on the staff of the New York Public Library selected several books by Wanda Gág for their annotated compilation, *Children's Books 1911–1986.* Like Moore, they were most enthusiastic about *Millions of Cats* and *Snow White and the Seven Dwarfs.*[39]

Children's literature textbooks such as *Children Experience Literature,*[40] *Children's Literature in the Elementary School,*[41] and Canadian professor Jon Stott's *Children's Literature from A to Z*[42] praise Gág's books. Zena Sutherland's 1986 revision of May Hill Arbuthnot's *Children and Books* considers *Millions of Cats,* along with Carl Sandburg's *Abe Lincoln Grows Up* and A. A. Milne's *Winnie the Pooh,* a "Twentieth Century Milestone."[43]

Biographical reference books about twentieth century children's literature and illustrations inevitably include Gág. For example, Michael Patrick Hearn wrote about "Wanda Gág" for the *Dictionary of Literary Biography: American Writers for Children, 1900–1960*[44] as well as for a pamphlet published by Coward-McCann on the occasion of the fiftieth anniversary of the first publication of *Millions of Cats.*[45] He updated the latter for the sixty-fifth anniversary year.[46]

Both Wanda Gág and Flavia Gag were included in *Illustrators of Children's Books 1744–1945.*[47] Excluding her published diary, the "Bibliography of Illustrators and Their Works" section listed Wanda Gág's other nine children's books.

Errors have crept into the biographical record about Wanda Gág. The entry in *Yesterday's Authors of Children's Books*[48] perpetuates some errors. Among them are the dates of her exhibit debut and marriage, the location of her home, and her place of death. She had exhibited at a branch of the New York Public Library twice before the Weyhe Gallery exhibit in 1926. Gág lived in rural New Jersey the last twenty years of her life, renting in New York City only on occasion. Gág married in 1943 at the age of fifty and she died in a New York City hospital. Mistakes occur also in another reference book, which erroneously states that Gág's mother was European, that *Tales from Grimm* was published the same year as *Gone Is Gone,* and that "in her late 30s she married and moved to New York City"[49]; Gág's mother was born in Harrisburg, Pennsylvania, and the American edition of *Tales from Grimm* was published in 1936 (the year following *Gone Is Gone*).

British children's book historians and critics also knew Gág's work. John Rowe Townsend, in his *Written for Children,* praised most of her books, but stated that *Nothing at All* "shows a total loss of cutting edge."[50] Marcus Crouch, writing for *Junior Bookshelf,* compared Gág favorably with earlier illustrators of the Brothers Grimm fairy tales (Crouch, 51–55). Margery Fisher identified the mice "Snippy and Snappy" in her *Who's Who in Children's Literature: A Treasury of the Familiar Characters of Childhood,*[51] but neglected Gág's other characters.

Among the names that any contemporary student of children's literature recognizes is that of Wanda Gág. Most textbooks on the subject include some information about her and inevitably cite *Millions of Cats* for special comment. Barbara Bader discusses Gág's work in her monumental book on the history of children's book illustration, *American Picturebooks from Noah's Ark to the Beast Within.* According to Bader, "Wanda Gág was as good as ready-made for the role of nursery celebrity."[52] Furthermore, she drew attention to Gág's continuing significance in her essay "A Second Look: *Millions of Cats.*" Even in its fiftieth anniversary year in 1978, the book was cited by Bader as possessing a special magic. In the same essay, she contended that *Gone Is Gone* was another masterpiece. The *Children's Literature Review* staff chose Gág as an entry in an early volume of reprinted reviews and articles.[53]

A Children's Literature Association (ChLA) committee selected *Millions of Cats* as one of the sixty classics or "touchstones" with which every teacher of children's literature should be acquainted. The organization, which is devoted to promoting serious scholarship and criticism in children's literature, appointed a committee to develop a "canon" or list of "distinguished children's books" [that] will allow us to better understand children's literature in general, and thus, to help children enjoy it more."[54] Several years later the association published three volumes about these major books. Picture books were treated in the third volume, which included *Millions of Cats*. The essayist highlighted Gág's success with "unity through repetition."[55]

Furthermore, historians and critics of children's literature as well as historians of American art and publishing also commented on Gág's importance to the field. Richard W. Cox's essay in *Minnesota History* places Gág in national historical context.[56] Carl Zigrosser, however, presented a negative evaluation of her art for the *Dictionary of American Biography,*[57] concluding that because she never painted in oils she was never truly significant as an artist. John Tebbel, a Yale University historian, noted in his book—published fifty years after Gág's first book—*A History of Book Publishing in the United States,* that *Millions of Cats* is "regarded by many as one of the most distinguished volumes of the century in this field. In making publishing history, it renewed the tradition of line drawing, which had been characteristic of quality magazines of the past, such as *Century, Harper's,* and *St. Nicholas"* (Tebbel, 172). A million copies of *Millions of Cats* had been sold by Gág's centenary year, 1993, sixty-five years after its publication; these were English-language hardcovers and paperbacks. Translations to a dozen other languages make the book accessible to children around the world.

Wanda Gág's books have remained in print and have appeared in new formats and translations over more than six decades since first published. In 1967, *The ABC Bunny* was still printed in gravure. The new Coward-McCann editor Alice Torrey wrote that it "can be done by only one printer and so it is [an] unbelievably expensive method of reproduction today" (Alice Torrey to Flavia Gag, 20 June 1967, Harm). Gág's picture books possessed such substantial texts that they sometimes appeared in print without illustrations. Anthologies that include her stories, for example, support the premise that she was a good writer and that her stories or translations of the Brothers Grimm fairy tales could stand alone. The *Anthology of Children's Literature,* edited by Edna Johnson, Evelyn R. Sickels, and Frances Clarke Sayers, contains *Millions of Cats, Gone Is Gone,* and several fairy tales translated by Gág.[58] Judith Saltman, in her editing of the sixth edition entitled *The Riverside Anthology of Children's Literature,* retained only *Millions of Cats.*[59] May Hill Arbuthnot's anthology also incorporates several Gág stories.[60] Houghton Mifflin and Scholastic reprinted *Millions of Cats,* while Houghton Mifflin and Macmillan reprinted *The ABC Bunny* in classroom texts.

Some of Gág's texts have been interpreted by artist Margot Tomes. She illustrated four individual fairy tales from *More Tales from Grimm,* originally translated and illustrated by Wanda Gág. These new editions appeared between 1978 and 1985 in a size similar to *Gone Is Gone.* Reviewing the first of these published, *Jorinda and Joringel,* for the *Horn Book,* Mary M. Burns noted "Gág's flowing translation of the folk tale . . . is the inspiration for a small, beautifully crafted book in which full-color illustrations alternating with detailed pen-and-ink drawings complement the ingenuousness of the narrative."[61] Other books illustrated by Tomes followed: *Wanda Gág's The Sorcerer's Apprentice* (1979), *The Six Swans* (1982), and *Earth Gnome* (1985).

Besides the traditional book style, Gág's works became available in other formats. Beginning in 1977 with *Millions of Cats,* Coward-McCann printed Gág books in paperback editions, which were cheaper. Paperbacks of *The ABC Bunny* followed in 1978; *Tales from Grimm* in 1981; and *The Funny Thing, Nothing at All,* and *Snippy and Snappy* in the 1990s. The Minnesota Historical Society published *Growing Pains* in paperback, with an added section, "Introduction to the Reprint Edition," in 1984.[62] On 1 September 1980 Coward, McCann and Geoghegan published *The Millions of Cats Day Book,*[63] with a different illustration as a headpiece for each month; it did not sell well and was soon remaindered. Other efforts followed. At the recommendation of narrator Owen Jordan, Weston Woods selected *Millions of Cats* for a filmstrip.[64] Later the Connecticut company converted the book and Gág's translation of "The Fisherman and His Wife" to video productions (Blanche Stout to the author, 15 August 1990, CLRC).

Besides being so accomplished herself, Wanda Gág inspired other Minnesotans to create productions based on her works. Heritage Productions produced *A Minnesota Childhood: Wanda Gág*[65] and *The Immigrant Experience: Anton Gag.*[66] Donald Betts, a music professor at Macalaster College in St. Paul, composed the lyrical "Portrait of the Artist as a Young Woman: Eleven Songs from the Diaries of Wanda Gág"[67] and "Three Sketches for Piano: After the Lithographs of Wanda Gág," which were first performed in 1990.[68]

Wanda Gág's books appealed to readers in other countries as well. Holt, Rinehart and Winston of Canada used *Tales from Grimm* in a classroom textbook. Faber and Faber in Great Britain published most of Gág's books within a year of the American publication dates. At that time, the American printer shipped plates across the Atlantic Ocean to the British printer. Translations of *Millions of Cats* also appeared in

Afrikaans, Danish, Hebrew, Italian, French, and Dutch. Franklin Books Programs arranged other editions for Third World Countries, including a Samoan edition of *Millions of Cats* and a Korean edition of *Gone Is Gone*. The Japanese publisher Fukuinkan Shoten reproduced *Millions of Cats,* while Iwanami Shoten published *Snippy and Snappy.* Three books were not published in the United Kingdom or elsewhere—*The Funny Thing, Growing Pains,* and *Three Gay Tales from Grimm.*

Aftermath for Family Members

Following Gág's death, her family and friends continued in their involvement with her legacy. Gág's husband, Earle Marshall Humphreys, served as the first executor of the estate. After he died suddenly in 1950 from a heart attack following a tennis match, Gág's brother-in-law Robert Janssen became executor of Gág's estate, a position he held for almost forty years (Janssen to Winnan, 7 October 1988, Winnan collection). Gary Harm, Gág's nephew, subsequently assumed that role. Howard, Gág's only brother and the person who had provided much of the handyman labor on her country home and property, died in 1961. Flavia, her youngest sister, who lived much of the time at All Creation, continued writing and drawing children's books and magazine articles. Nonetheless, she never reached her oldest sister's zenith. Altogether Flavia wrote and illustrated nine books and made drawings for thirteen others. Among the latter was *The Wiley Woodchucks,*[69] written by Wanda Gág's girlhood friend Alma Schmidt Scott under the pseudonym of Georgia Travers. The episode, based on Scott's visit with her two daughters to Wanda Gág's home, describes two woodchucks who invade the garden at All Creation. Scott used the real names of the people in the text and referred to the woodchucks as Pudgy and Charles. This book was published in the fall of 1946, after Gág's death in June of that year.

As well as illustrating books for Coward-McCann, Flavia worked for Harper, Holt, McKay, Random House, and Charles Scribner's Sons. She eventually followed her sister's advice that she write something based on her childhood. *A Wish for Mimi* was published more than a decade after Wanda Gág's death.[70] In this fictional story, a fatherless family of six girls and one boy live in a large house in a small German town. The house had a coal furnace and running water only in the sink. The heroine Mimi's greatest desire is to have a bathtub with a hot-water tap. Author-illustrator Flavia changed the family's ethnicity from German to French-American. Her illustrations portray the artifacts in the Gag home. The chapter "A Tent for a Home" recalls the summer after the New Ulm house was sold when some of the Gag children camped in a pasture on the Dehn farm in Waterville, Minnesota. Both the camping episode and the illustration of the Minneapolis apartment house to which some Gág siblings later moved are based on Flavia's memory. In a presentation copy of the book, Flavia inscribed, "This book required no research; I had only to go into reverie and recall the many incidents of my childhood, all still very vivid to me" (CLRC). Alice Torrey, then the children's book editor at Coward-McCann, was not interested in Flavia's manuscript for the biography of her famous sister (Torrey to Flavia Gag, 3 May 1960, Harm). Flavia Gag lived until age seventy-one. She died from cancer in 1978.

Wanda Gág's Inspiration Continues

Authors, illustrators, and editors in succeeding generations continue to be inspired by Wanda Gág and her work. Eleanor Cameron, the author of numerous children's books, including the 1974 National Book Award winner *The Court of the Stone Children*, cites Gág in her literary criticism.[71] In her book *The Green and Burning Tree*, she devotes an entire chapter to Gág." Moreover, she recommended that the children's magazine *Cricket* reprint Gág's "The Cry-Away Bird," a project that came to fruition in 1976.[72] The story also appeared in a Canadian reading program and will be reprinted in an American textbook series. Because Cameron wanted contemporary children to be acquainted with Wanda Gág, she wrote an article in the same issue of *Cricket* about the author-illustrator's childhood experiences—"I Am Really Alive"—with which youngsters could relate.[73]

Children wrote letters to Wanda Gág during her life, and some continued writing long after her death. In one letter a girl in Massachusetts suggested that Gág write a story about a little kitten. Gág's notation on the letter indicates that she answered it four months later and sent along a "story letter" (Joan Maguire to Gág, 6 May 1945, CLRC). A child from Ohio queried, "Why didn't you call the funny thing a dragon?" (Jorinda Briggs to Gág, 17 January 1967, CLRC). A boy from Chicago asked, "How did you get the idea of making an invisible dog [in *Nothing at All*] as a white ball?" (Eddie Mercado to Gág, 13 March 1973, CLRC). And a girl from Brooklyn commented, "The reason I enjoyed this story [*Gone Is Gone*] is because it fits in with times of today when women and men are changing their roles in the house" (Tisha Passalacqua to Gág, 1 October 1972, CLRC).

Awards came to Wanda Gág posthumously. In 1977, the University of Wisconsin School of Education designated *Millions of Cats* as a Lewis Carroll Shelf Award recipient, worthy to sit beside *Alice in Wonderland.* The University of Minnesota bestowed the 1977 Kerlan Award on Wanda Gág, "in recognition of singular attainments in the creation of children's literature and in appreciation for generous donation of unique resources to the Kerlan Collection for the study of children's literature." Flavia Gag accepted the award and spoke at the ceremony.

Time was kinder to the Disney *Snow White and the Seven Dwarfs* film and its plethora of books than to Gág's version. In *Films in America, 1926–1969,* the authors state that the first feature-length cartoon by Walt Disney "remains three decades later his most popular of that genre with audiences, and its biggest grosser."[74] The controversy about Disney's interpretation continued. Two well-known scholars disagreed with one another. Stith Thompson, founder of the Folklore Department at Indiana University, stated in *The Folktale* that "Walt Disney was particularly successful in catching the traditional conception of the dwarf."[75] In contrast to the American scholar Thompson, C. S. Lewis, the author and professor at Cambridge University, recalled, "I fell deeply under the spell of Dwarfs—the old bright-hooded, snowy bearded dwarfs we had in those days before Arthur Rackham sublimed, or Walt Disney vulgarized, the earthmen."[76] Nevertheless, in 1988, when Congress passed the National Film Preservation Act, the Disney film was among the twenty-five placed on the National Film Registry. It is ironic that about fifty years after children's librarians panned Walt Disney's *Snow White and the Seven Dwarfs,* the Library of Congress motion picture staff agreed with the National Film Preservation Board's selection of that film.[77] The only other film created especially for children on the list was *Wizard of Oz.*

Along with the film, which is now available in video, newly illustrated books have overshadowed Gág's version. The story of Snow White has engaged many illustrators during the past fifty years. In 1962, editor Michael Di Capua contacted Maurice Sendak about illustrating a collection of the Brothers Grimm fairy tales, which he envisioned being translated by Randall Jarrell. After the poet died in 1965, Lore Segal continued the translation project. Sendak traveled to Germany in 1971 to visit the areas where the Brothers Grimm had collected the fairy tales more than 150 years before. In contrast to Gág's spending seven weeks on all the illustrations for her edition, Sendak worked more than four months on his single illustration for "Snow White," and it was the last one he drew for that book. "The more familiar the tale, Sendak discovered, the more difficult it was to find just the right moment to illustrate."[78] In fall 1973, exactly thirty-five years after the publication of Gág's *Snow White and the Seven Dwarfs*, Farrar, Strauss and Giroux published the Jarrell translation as *The Juniper Tree and Other Tales from Grimm*, illustrated by Maurice Sendak.[79] Since then, Nancy Ekholm Burkert, Trina Schart Hyman, and many other illustrators have created notable interpretations of Snow White. Nevertheless, the New York Public Library staff concluded in 1986 that Gág's *Snow White and the Seven Dwarfs* is "the best version of this tale for reading aloud to young children" (*Children's Books 1911–1986*, 21).

Several events occurred during the Gág centennial year in Minnesota. Her nephew Gary Harm cut the birthday cake at the University of Minnesota celebration and a party was held simultaneously at the Wanda Gág House in New Ulm on 13 March 1993. The Brown County Historical Society mounted an exhibit opening 1 May to last through 1994. The Wanda Gág House Association hosted a banquet in Turner Hall in New Ulm on May 1; Gág's nephew Gary and niece Barbara Jean were present. This was the building where the child Wanda had accompanied her father when he decorated the interior and painted scenery almost a century before. The Minnesota Historical Society exhibited Gág's drawings and prints at the J. J. Hill House in the late spring and summer; some were selected for further showing at the ten-day Minnesota State Fair concluding on Labor Day. In July 1994 an exhibit of Gág's children's book illustrations from the Kerlan Collection, along with those of two others—Virginia Lee Burton and Marie Hall Ets—opened in Tokyo, Japan, sponsored by the Book Globe Company. The Frederick R. Weisman Art Museum at the University of Minnesota in Minneapolis is to sponsor a traveling exhibit to open in 1995.

Conclusion

Wanda Gág made an enormous impact on the American children's book field, and thereby on its future. Furthermore, she remains influential for today's artists and writers of children's books, many of whom read her books as children or adults. All ten of her books remain in print forty and fifty years after their initial presentation; and new translations, reproductions, reprints, audiovisual media editions, and anthologies keep the stories alive. Children's literature critics, journalists, and art historians continue to write about her. Audur H. Winnan's *Wanda Gág: A Catalogue Raisonné of the Prints*, published in 1993, furthers Gág's reputation as an artist.[80] *Millions of Cats* undoubtedly will continue to appear on the most selective lists of important American children's books. Children read *Millions of Cats* and other books by Gág in their own language in many countries.

Like Cinderella, Wanda Gág was born into a nurturing and supportive family environment, which collapsed before she reached maturity. In her translation of the Grimm "Cinderella" fairy tale, Gág elaborated on the hard work Cinderella completed before attending the ball. Gág, too, worked arduously and consistently toward her goal to become a well-known artist. Adulation and fairy-tale-like success followed a long preparatory time of self-denial and hard work. Gág claimed that she kept her artistic standards for children's books as high as for her drawings and prints. She expressed satisfaction with her children's books. Wanda Gág fulfilled her father's challenge, too, to finish what he had started—to become an important artist—and she achieved it in her own way.

Notes and References

Chapter One

1. June Holmquist, *They Chose Minnesota* (St. Paul: Minnesota Historical Society, 1981), 167.
2. Gág to Minneapolis Public Library, 26 October 1944, Minneapolis Public Library Children's Department.
3. Alma [Schmidt] Scott, *Wanda Gág: The Story of an Artist* (Minneapolis: University of Minnesota Press, 1949), 47; hereafter cited in text.
4. Wanda Gág, *Growing Pains: Diaries and Drawings for the Years 1908–1917* (New York: Coward-McCann, 1940), xix; hereafter cited in text as *Growing.*
5. Gág, Diary 44, Autumn 1928. All of Gág's diaries are located in the Wanda Gág Collection, Special Collections, Van Pelt Library, University of Pennsylvania, Philadelphia. (Diary entries are hereafter cited in text; diary number is supplied when available. References to other holdings in the Van Pelt Library are also cited in text, followed by the abbreviation VP.) Gág to Scott, 14 May 1944, Alma Scott Papers, Minnesota Historical Society; the society is hereafter cited in text as MHS.
6. Gág to Edgar Hermann, 9 June 1914, Elizabeth Cowie Private Collection, St. Paul, Minn.
7. Dehn's first name was originally spelled Adolphe; he later changed it to Adolf and used this version for professional purposes. This latter spelling is used throughout the book.
8. Jean Sherwood Rankin, *A Child's Book of Folklore: Mechanics of Written English; a Drill in the Use of Caps and Points through the Rimes of Mother Goose,* illus. Wanda Gág (Minneapolis: Augsburg Publishing House, 1917).
9. Lawrence Campbell to Audur H. Winnan, 23 August 1989, Audur H. Winnan Private Collection.
10. Gág to Harold A. Larrabee, August 1923, Children's Literature Research Collections, University of Minnesota, Minneapolis; this collection is hereafter cited in text as CLRC.
11. Wanda Gág, Notebook of Ideas, Wanda Gág Papers, Philadelphia Museum of Art.
12. Gág, form letter distributed by Coward-McCann, 1939(?), CLRC.
13. *Pioneer* 4 (1923): 25–28.
14. Wanda Gág's "Blaa Books" are housed in the CLRC.
15. Wanda Gág, *Batiking at Home: A Handbook for Beginners* (New York: Crowell, 1925).
16. Wanda Gág, "These Modern Women: A Hotbed of Feminists," *Nation* 124 (1927): 691–93.

17. Wand Gág, *Millions of Cats* (New York: Coward-McCann, 1928); hereafter cited in text as *Millions*.

18. Flavia Gag, "Snoopy and Snooky," *American Junior Red Cross News* 39 (March 1958): 20–23.

19. Marya Mannes, "Wanda Gág: Individualist," *Creative Art* 1 (December 1927): xxix.

20. Anne Herendeen, "Wanda Gág: The True Story of a Dynamic Young Artist Who Won't Be Organized," *Century* 116 (August 1928): 427; hereafter cited in text.

21. Winifred and Frances Kirkland, *Girls Who Became Artists* (New York: Harper, 1934), 9.

22. Spencer Kellogg, Jr., *Autumn Embers* (Eden, N.Y.: Aries Press, 1927).

23. Spencer Kellogg, Jr., *The Oak by Waters of Rowan* (Eden, N.Y.: Aries Press, 1927).

24. Wanda Gág, *The Funny Thing* (New York: Coward-McCann, 1929); hereafter cited in text as *Funny*.

25. Wanda Gág, *Snippy and Snappy* (New York: Coward-McCann, 1931); hereafter cited in text as *Snippy*.

26. Wanda Gág, *The ABC Bunny* (New York: Coward-McCann, 1933); hereafter cited in text as *ABC*.

27. Wanda Gág, *Gone Is Gone, or The Story of a Man Who Wanted to Do Housework* (New York: Coward-McCann, 1935); hereafter cited in text as *Gone*.

28. Wanda Gág, *Nothing at All* (New York: Coward-McCann, 1941); hereafter cited in text as *Nothing*.

29. Jakob and Wilhelm Grimm, *Tales from Grimm,* trans. and illus. Wanda Gág (New York: Coward-McCann, 1936); hereafter cited in text as *Tales*.

30. Jakob and Wilhelm Grimm, *Snow White and the Seven Dwarfs,* translated and illustrated by Wanda Gág (New York: Coward-McCann, 1938); hereafter cited in text as *Snow White*.

31. Jakob and Wilhelm Grimm, *Three Gay Tales from Grimm,* trans. and illus. Wanda Gág (New York: Coward-McCann, 1943); hereafter cited in text as *Three Tales*.

32. Jakob and Wilhelm Grimm, *More Tales from Grimm,* trans. and illus. Wanda Gág (New York: Coward-McCann, 1947); hereafter cited in text as *More Tales*.

33. Michael Wigglesworth, *The Day of Doom, or A Poetical Description of the Great and Last Judgment, with Other Poems,* ed. and intro. Kenneth B. Mudock, with drawings adapted from early New England gravestones by Wanda Gág (New York: Spiral Press, 1929).

34. Thomas R. Coward, "Wanda Gág," *Four Star Final* 11 (January 1947): 2.

35. Wanda Gág, draft for Guggenheim Fellowship Application, 9 January 1939, CLRC.

36. Wanda Gág, "I Wanted to Draw," *Story Parade* 6 (November 1941): 42–44.

37. Dorothy Rowe, *The Begging Deer and Other Stories of Japanese Children,* illus. Lynd Ward (New York: Macmillan, 1928).

38. Lynd Ward, *God's Man: A Novel in Woodcuts* (New York: J. Cape & H. Smith, 1929).

39. Rockwell Kent, *Wilderness* (New York: Putnam, 1920).

40. Rockwell Kent, *N by E* (New York: Harcourt, 1930).

41. Flavia Gag Diary, 10 March 1945, Gary and Norma Harm Private Collection, Minneapolis, Minn.; the collection is hereafter cited in the text as Harm.

42. Flavia Gag, *Sing a Song of Seasons: Songs and Pictures* (New York: Coward-McCann, 1936).

43. Alma Schmidt Scott, *The Story of Kattor,* pseud. Georgia Travers, illus. Flavia Gag (New York: Coward-McCann, 1939).

Chapter Two

1. Hellmut Lehmann-Haupt, *The Book in America: A History of the Making and Selling of Books in the United States* (New York: Bowker, 1952), 374.

2. Mary Calletto Rife to Jane Botham, 11 June 1986, in Association of Library Services to Children's Division of the American Library Association files, Chicago headquarters.

3. Anne Carroll Moore, *The Three Owls: A Book About Children's Books, Their Authors, Artists, and Critics,* vol. 1 (New York: Macmillan, 1925), vol. 2 (New York: Coward-McCann, 1928), vol. 3 (New York: Coward-McCann, 1931).

4. "American Book Production 1928," *Publishers Weekly* 115 (19 January 1929): 275.

5. Ernestine Evans, "The Red Horse Trots Again," *Four Star Final-Juvenile Supplement* 8 (Fall 1944): 5.

6. Ernestine Evans, "Wanda Gág," *Four Star Final-Juvenile Supplement* 10 (August–September 1946): 4.

7. Ernestine Evans, "Wanda Gág as Writer, *Horn Book* 23 (May–June 1947): 182.

8. Gág to George Biddle, 1 November 1928, George Biddle Papers, Archives of American Art, New York City.

9. Anne Carroll Moore, "A Distinguished Picture Book," *New York Herald Tribune Books,* 9 September 1928, 9.

10. Elizabeth Coatsworth, "Reviews: *Millions of Cats,*" *Saturday Review of Literature* 5 (22 September 1928): 149.

11. Ernestine Evans, "This Year's Crop," *Nation* 21 (21 November 1928): 547–48.

12. "The Nation's Honor Roll for 1928," *Nation* 22 (9 January 1929): 35.

13.   Augusta Baker and Ellin Greene, *Storytelling: Art and Technique* (New York: Bowker, 1977), 52.

14.   Irene Smith, *A History of the Newbery and Caldecott Medals* (New York: Viking, 1957), 43; hereafter cited in text.

15.   John Tebbel, *A History of Book Publishing in the United States* vol. 3 (New York: Bowker, 1978), 562; hereafter cited in text.

16.   Rose Dobbs, "Ten Years of Publishing Children's Books," *Horn Book* 14 (September–October 1938): 317.

17.   "Books Published January to December," *Publisher and Bookseller*, 3 January 1930, 17.

18.   Wanda Gág, *Millioner af Katte*, trans. B. B. Moller (Copenhagen: P. Haase, 1948).

19.   Wanda Gág, *Millioner af Katte*, trans. Anine Rud (Copenhagen: Gyldendal, 1968).

20.   Wanda Gág, *Millioner af Katte*, trans. Nanna Gyldenkaerne (Copenhagen: Agertoft, 1987).

21.   Louis Untermeyer, *Blue Rhine, Black Forest: A Hand- and Day-Book* (New York: Harcourt Brace, 1930).

22.   Barbara Bader, *American Picturebooks from Noah's Ark to the Beast Within* (New York: Macmillan; London: Collier Macmillan, 1976), 37.

Chapter Three

1.   Gág to Lewis Gannett, May 1929, in Lewis Gannett Papers, Rare Books and Manuscripts, Houghton Library, Harvard University.

2.   Lynd Ward, "Some Picture Books of the Year," *New York Herald Tribune Books*, 17 November 1929, 9.

3.   "Wanda Gág—Graver and Illustrator," *Index of Twentieth Century Artists* 3 (July 1936): 293–94.

4.   Muriel Fuller, "Some Books for Children," *New York World*, 1 December 1929, 11.

5.   Rachel Field, *Hitty, Her First Hundred Years* (New York: Macmillan, 1929).

6.   Rachel Field, "A Sheaf of Picture Books," *Saturday Review of Literature* 6 (16 November 1929): 403.

7.   Muriel Fuller, "Rose Dobbs of Coward-McCann," *Publishers Weekly* 84 (22 October 1938): 1522.

8.   Anne Carroll Moore, "Round the World in Children's Books," *New York Times Book Review*, 15 November 1931, 2.

9.   Lynd Ward, "Two Field Mice," *New York Herald Tribune Books*, 15 November 1931, 2.

10.   Rachel Field, "Picture Books Ahoy," *Saturday Review of Literature* 8 (14 November 1931): 296.

11.   Laura Adams Armer, *Waterless Mountain* (New York: Longmans, 1931).

12. Asta, Dehli, and Flavia Gag. *Sue Sew and Sew* (New York: Coward-McCann, 1931).

13. Walter D. Edmonds, *The Matchlock Gun,* illus. Paul Lantz (New York: Dodd, Mead, 1941).

14. Walter A. Edmonds, *Uncle Ben's Whale,* illus. William Gropper (New York: Dodd, Mead, 1955).

15. Wanda Gág, *Wanda Gág's Story Book: Millions of Cats, The Funny Thing, Snippy and Snappy* (New York: Coward-McCann, 1932).

16. "Communications," *Publishers Weekly* 121 (8 June 1932): 2418.

17. Emma L. Brock, "Children's Librarians' Notebook," *Library Journal* 58 (1933): 518.

18. Anne T. Eaton, "This Year's Books for Children," *New York Times Book Review,* 12 November 1933, 21.

19. Alice Dalgliesh, "Picture Books: *The ABC Bunny,*" *Saturday Review of Literature* 10 (1933): 279.

20. Elizabeth Morrow, *Beast, Bird, and Fish: An Animal Alphabet,* illus. Rene d'Harnoncourt, music Eberhard d'Harnoncourt (New York: Knopf, 1933).

21. Cornelia Meigs, *Invincible Louisa* (New York: Little, Brown, 1933).

Chapter Four

1. Caroline Hewins, *Books for the Young: A Guide for Parents and Children* (New York: F. Leypoldt, 1882).

2. Jakob and Wilhelm Grimm, *Grimm's Fairy Tales,* sel. and retold Githa Sowerby, illus. Millicent Sowerby (New York: F. A. Stokes, 1910).

3. Jakob and Wilhelm Grimm, *Grimm's Fairy Tales,* trans. Margaret Hunt, illus. John B. Gruelle (New York: Cupples and Leon, 1914).

4. Jakob and Wilhelm Grimm, *Grimm's Fairy Tales,* trans. Ernest Beeson, illus. George Soper (New York: George H. Doran, 1924).

5. Jakob and Wilhelm Grimm, *German Popular Stories* vol. 1, illus. George Cruikshank (London: C. Baldwin, 1823), vol. 2, illus. George Cruikshank (London: James Robins, 1826).

6. Marie L. Shedlock, *The Art of the Storyteller* (New York: D. Appleton, 1927).

7. Mary Gould Davis, "The Story-Teller's Art," *Horn Book* 10 (May 1934): 137–43.

8. Wanda Gág, "I Like Fairy Tales," *Horn Book* 15 (March–April, 1939): 75–80.

9. Wanda Gág, in May Lamberton Becker, "Parents: Let No Child Go Hungry for Books," *New York Herald Tribune Books,* 13 November 1932, sec. 10, p. 1.

10. *Candle-Light Stories,* sel. and ed. Veronica S. Hutchinson, drawings Lois Lenski (New York: Minton, Balch, 1928).

11. Laura Benet, "Joyous Wisdom in Pictures and Stories," *New York Herald Tribune Books,* 17 November 1935, vii, 11.

12. Anne T. Eaton, "New Books for Girls and Boys," *New York Times Book Review*, 6 October 1935, 10.

13. Marjorie F. Potter, "Children's Librarians Notebook," *Library Journal* 60 (1 November 1935): 857.

14. Carol Ryrie Brink, *Caddie Woodlawn* (New York: Macmillan, 1935).

15. Wanda Gág, "The Cryaway Bird," *Delineator* 126 (May 1935): 39.

16. Wanda Gág, "A Man Who Wanted to Do Housework: An Old Tale Retold and Illustrated by Wanda Gág," *Child Life* 14 (December 1935): 542–45, 587.

17. *Children's Books Suggested as Holiday Gifts* (New York: New York Public Library, 1936).

18. Anne T. Eaton, "The Changing Art of Writing for Children," *New York Times Book Review*, 15 November 1936, 12.

19. May Lamberton Becker, "Old Fairy-Stories in Their New Dresses," *New York Herald Tribune Books*, 15 November 1936, 9.

20. Marcus Crouch, "Through Peasant Eyes," *Junior Bookshelf* 26 (March 1962): 53.

21. *Boston Evening Transcript*, "A Miscellany of Fiction as the New Year Dawns," 2 January 1937.

22. Ruth Sawyer, *Roller Skates* (New York: Viking, 1936).

23. Humbert Wolfe, "Golden Lads and Lasses," *Observer*, 5 December 1937.

24. "A New Translation of Grimm," *Junior Bookshelf* 2 (October 1937): 28.

25. *Walt Disney's Famous Seven Dwarfs* (Hollywood: Walt Disney Enterprises, 1938).

26. *Walt Disney's Famous Seven Dwarfs* (Racine, Wis.: Whitman, 1938).

27. *Walt Disney's Snow White and the Seven Dwarfs* (Racine, Wis.: Whitman, 1938).

28. *The Story of Walt Disney's Snow White and the Seven Dwarfs*, based on the Walt Disney motion picture, by the staff of the Walt Disney studios, authorized ed. (Racine, Wis.: Whitman, 1938).

29. Anne Carroll Moore, "The Three Owls' Notebook," *Horn Book* 14 (January–February 1938): 32.

30. Anne Carroll Moore, "The Three Owls Notebook," *Horn Book* 14 (May–June 1938): 173.

31. Louise Seaman Bechtel, "From the Picture Book Package," *Saturday Review of Literature* 19 (19 November 1938): 18.

32. Anne T. Eaton, "The New Books for Young Readers," *New York Times Book Review*, 7 August 1938, 10.

33. May Lamberton Becker, "Books for Young People," *New York Herald Tribune Books*, 13 November 1938, 9.

34. Thomas Handforth, *Mei Li* (New York: Doubleday, 1938); Elizabeth Enright, *Thimble Summer* (New York: Rinehart, 1938).

35. Eleanor Graham, "The Season's Children's Books, Great Richness and Variety," *Bookseller*, 1 September 1938, 731.

36. "The Publisher and Bookseller Classified List; Children's Books and Minor Fiction," *Bookseller,* 29 September 1938, 872.

37. Graham Bell, "Art and Artiface for Nursery Readers," *New Statesmen and Nation* 16 (10 December 1938): 980.

38. Ruth Bryan Owen, *The Castle in the Silver Wood and Other Scandinavian Fairy Tales,* illus. Marc Simont (New York: Dodd, Mead, 1939).

39. Gág, form letter distributed by Coward-McCann, 1940(?), CLRC.

Chapter Five

1. Paul Klee, *Tagebucher von Paul Klee 1898–1918,* ed. Felix Klee (Cologne: Verlag M. DuMont Schauberg, 1956).

2. Thomas Craven, *The Treasury of American Prints: A Selection of One Hundred Etchings and Lithographs by the Foremost Living Artists* (New York: Simon and Schuster, 1939).

3. Thomas Craven, "The Diary of a Working Artist," *New York Herald Tribune Books,* 29 September 1940, ix, 2.

4. Anne Carroll Moore, "The Three Owls Notebook," *Horn Book* 16 (September–October 1940): 339.

5. M. H., "Noted Illustrator Publishes Diaries," *Boston Evening Transcript,* 5 October 1940, Part 5, 2.

6. Frances Margaret Fox, *True Monkey Stories,* illus. Tibor Gergely (Boston: Lothrop Lee & Shepard, 1941).

7. Anne T. Eaton, "Invisible Dog," *New York Times,* 2 November 1941, 38.

8. "New Books: For Children under Nine: *Nothing at All," Junior Bookshelf* 6 (July 1942): 95.

9. Robert McCloskey, *Make Way for Ducklings* (New York: Viking, 1941); Walter Edmonds, *The Matchlock Gun,* illus. Paul Lantz (New York: Dodd, 1941).

10. May Lamberton Becker, "Picture Books for the Little Folks, *New York Herald Tribune Weekly Book Review,* 14 November 1943, sec. 6, p. 2.

11. Mary Gould Davis, "Folk and Fanciful Tales: *Three Gay Tales from Grimm," Saturday Review of Literature* 26 (13 November 1943), 27.

12. "Children's Books for Christmas," *New Yorker* 19 (4 December 1943): 132.

13. Fritz Eichenberg, "New Picture Books: *Three Gay Tales from Grimm," Horn Book* 20 (January–February 1944): 21.

14. James Thurber, *Many Moons,* illus. Louis Slobodkin (New York: Harcourt, 1943); Esther Forbes, *Johnny Tremain* (Boston: Houghton Mifflin, 1943).

15. "Three Gay Tales," *Junior Bookshelf* 10 (October 1946): 130.

16. Johan Egilsrud, *Pond Image* (Minneapolis: Lund Press, 1942).

17. "Wanda and Gág," "Going to the Butcher Shop," "Going Down to Grandma's," and "Paper Dolls" are located in the CLRC.
18. "Snowshoveling" is in the Harm collection.
19. "Grab Bag," "Playing Dentist," and "Sandstone" are in the Van Pelt Library.
20. "Characters Children Love," *Look* 8 (26 December 1944): 34–35.
21. Jakob and Wilhelm Grimm, *Grimm's Fairy Tales,* trans. and illus. Fritz Kredel (New York: Stackpole, 1937).
22. "East of the Sun and West of the Moon," illus. Wanda Gág, in *The Book of Knowledge: The Children's Encyclopedia* 15 (New York: Grolier Society, 1947): 5439–45.
23. Ellen Lewis Buell, "Fantasy: *More Tales from Grimm,*" *New York Times Book Review,* 16 November 1947, 5.
24. Anne Carroll Moore, "The Three Owl's Notebook," *Horn Book Magazine* 23 (September–October 1947): 347.
25. May Lamberton Becker, "Books for Young People, Where Fancy Is Free to Roam in Beauty," *New York Herald Tribune Weekly Book Review,* 16 November 1947, 6.
26. William Pene du Bois, *The Twenty-One Balloons* (New York: Viking, 1947); Roger Duvoisin, *White Snow Bright Snow* (New York: Lothrop, 1947).

Chapter Six

1. Bruno Bettelheim, *The Uses of Enchantment: The Meaning and Importance of Fairy Tales* (New York: Knopf, 1976), 10.
2. *Who's Who in American Art* (Washington, D.C.: American Federation of Arts, 1937), 159.
3. *Who's Who in America, 1941* (Chicago: Marquis, 1942).
4. *American Art Annual,* vols. 26, 28, 29, 30 (Washington, D.C.: American Federation of Arts, 1929, 1931, 1932, 1933).
5. Daniel Trowbridge Mallett, *Mallett's Index of Artists* (New York: Bowker, 1935), 150.
6. Anne T. Eaton, "New Children's Books: *Snippy and Snappy,*" *New York Times Book Review,* 1 November 1931, 24.
7. Ruth Sawyer, *The Way of the Storyteller* (New York: Viking, 1942), 181.
8. *Children's Book Show, 1920–1952* (New York: American Institute of Graphic Arts, 1952).
9. Elisabeth Luther Cary, "Casual Impressions of Modernism" *American Magazine of Art* 21 (August 1930): 424.
10. Elisabeth Luther Cary, "Peggy Bacon and Wanda Gág," *Prints* 1 (March 1931): 13–24.
11. Carl Zigrosser, "Modern American Graphic Art," *Creative Art* 9 (November 1931): 369–74.

12. Carl Zigrosser, "Graphic Art in America," *Studio* 127 (June 1944): 188–92.

13. Carl Zigrosser, *The Artist in America* (New York: Knopf, 1942), xv.

14. Winifred and Frances Kirkland, "She Followed Her Bent," *Classmate: A Paper for Young People* 40 (4 March 1933): 2.

15. "Wanda Gág," *Junior Book of Authors*, ed. Stanley Jasspon Kunitz and Howard Haycraft (New York: H. W. Wilson, 1934): 159–60.

16. "Wanda Gág," *Twentieth Century Authors: A Biographical Dictionary of Modern Literature*, ed. Stanley J. Kunitz and Howard Haycraft (New York: H. W. Wilson, 1942), 509.

17. Carmen Nelson Richards and Genevieve Rose Breen, eds., *Minnesota Writers: A Collection of Autobiographical Stories by Minnesota Prose Writers* (Minneapolis: Lund Press, 1945).

18. Ellis Credle, *Down, Down the Mountain* and *Across the Cotton Patch* (New York: Nelson, 1934, 1935).

19. Virginia Lee Burton, *The Little House* (Boston: Houghton Mifflin, 1942); Marie Hall Ets, *Nine Days to Christmas* (New York: Viking, 1959).

20. Barbara Bader, "A Second Look: Millions of Cats," *Horn Book* 55 (October 1978): 540.

21. B[ertha] E. M[ahony], "Two Artists," *Horn Book* 22 (September–October 1946): 331.

22. Anne Carroll Moore, "Art for Life's Sake," *Horn Book* 23 (May–June 1947): 157.

23. Alma Scott, "Wanda Gág," *Horn Book* 23 (May–June 1947): 159–67.

24. Carl Zigrosser, "Wanda Gág, Artist," *Horn Book* 23 (May–June 1947): 170–81.

25. Ernestine Evans, "Wanda Gág as Writer," in *A Horn Book Sampler: On Children's Books and Reading, Selected from Twenty-Five Years of The Horn Book Magazine 1924–1948*, ed. Norma R. Fryatt (Boston: Horn Book, 1959), 34–38.

26. Rose Dobbs, "Wanda Gág, Fellow Worker," *Horn Book* 23 (May–June 1947): 189–93.

27. Lynd Ward, The Biggest Bear (Boston: Houghton Mifflin, 1952); and "Wanda Gág, Fellow-Artist," *Horn Book* 23 (May–June 1947): 194–97.

28. Earle Marshall Humphreys, selector and ed., "Letters from Children to Wanda Gág," *Horn Book* 23 (May–June, 1947): 198–205.

29. Jakob and Wilhelm Grimm, "The Cat and the Fox," trans. and illus. Wanda Gág, *Horn Book* 23 (May–June 1947): 206–7.

30. "Prints by Wanda Gág," *Bulletin of the Minneapolis Institute of Arts* 35 (7 December 1946): 153–59.

31. "Wanda Gág: Catalogue of the Harold A. Larrabee Collection of Wanda Gág" (1976), typescript in the Library, Graduate School of Library Science Library, Harry Ransom Center, the University of Texas at Austin; Carol Spencer Howard, "Wanda Gág Collection in Texas," *Horn Book* 55 (October 1978): 582–83.

32. *Three Women Artists: Gág, Greenman, and Mairs* (Minneapolis: University Gallery, 1980).

33. Robert M. Walker, "Wanda Gág: The Story of an Artist," *Horn Book* 27 (January–February 1951): 48–53.

34. Alma Scott, "Wanda Gág," in *Notable American Women 1607–1950* vol. 2, ed. Edward T. James, Janet Wilson James, and Paul S. Boyer (Cambridge: Belknap Press of Harvard University Press, 1971), 1–2.

35. Beatrice J. Hurley, "Wanda Gág—Artist, Author," *Elementary English* 32 (October 1955): 347–54.

36. Jane P. Renshaw, "Wanda Wouldn't Stop Drawing," *Trails for Juniors* 9 (October, 1950): 6–7.

37. Mary Ann Nord, "Wanda Gág Makes a Wish Come True," *Roots* 8 (Winter 1980): 16–23.

38. Virginia Haviland, "Search for the Real Thing among the 'Millions and Billions and Trillions' of Books," *Library Journal* 86 (15 December 1961): 4332.

39. *Children's Books 1911–1986: Favorite Children's Books from the Branch Collections of the New York Public Library* (New York: New York Public Library, 1986); hereafter cited in text as *Children's Books 1911–1986*.

40. Bernard J. Lonsdale and Helen K. Macintosh, *Children Experience Literature* (New York: Random House, 1973), 188, 228–29.

41. Charlotte Huck, *Children's Literature in the Elementary School,* 3d ed. (New York: Holt, 1979).

42. Jon C. Stott, *Children's Literature from A to Z: A Guide for Parents and Teachers* (New York: McGraw-Hill, 1984), 117–19.

43. Zena Sutherland, *Children and Books,* 7th ed. (Glenview, Ill.: Scott Foresman, 1986), 78.

44. Michael Patrick Hearn, "Wanda Gág," *Dictionary of Literary Biography: American Writers for Children, 1900–1960,* vol. 22, ed. John Cech (Detroit: Gale, 1983), 179–91.

45. Michael Patrick Hearn, *50 Years of Wanda Gág's "Millions of Cats," 1928–1978* (New York: Coward-McCann, 1978).

46. Michael Patrick Hearn, *65 Years of Wanda Gág's "Millions of Cats," 1928–1993* (New York: Coward, McCann & Geoghegan, 1993.)

47. Bertha E. Mahony, Louise Payson Latimer, and Beulah Folmsbee, *Illustrators of Children's Books, 1744–1945* (Boston: Horn Book, 1947), 309–10, 411.

48. "Wanda Gág," *Yesterday's Authors of Books for Children,* vol. 1, ed. Anne Commire (Detroit: Gale Research, 1977), 135–43.

49. Humphrey Carpenter and Mari Prichard, *The Oxford Companion to Children's Literature* (New York: Oxford University Press, 1984), 194.

50. John Rowe Townsend, *Written for Children: An Outline of English-Language Children's Literature,* 3d rev. ed. (New York: Lippincott, 1987), 179.

51. Marjorie Fisher, *Who's Who in Children's Literature* (New York: Holt, 1975), 326–27.

52. Barbara Bader, *American Picturebooks from Noah's Ark to the Beast Within* (New York: Macmillan, 1976), 32.

53. "Wanda Gág," *Children's Literature Review,* vol. 4 (Detroit: Gale Research, 1982), 78–88.

54. Perry Nodelman, "Touchstones," *Touchstones: A List of Distinguished Children's Books* (West Lafayette, Ind.: Children's Literature Association, n.d.), 2.

55. Mary Kissel, "Wanda Gág's *Millions of Cats*: Unity Through Repetition," in *Touchstones: Reflections on the Best in Children's Literature,* vol. 3, ed. Perry Nodelman (West Lafayette, Ind.: Children's Literature Association, 1989), 54–62.

56. Richard W. Cox, "Wanda Gág: The Bite of the Picture Book," *Minnesota History* 44 (Fall 1975): 238–54.

57. Carl Zigrosser, "Wanda Gág," in *Dictionary of American Biography, Supplement Four, 1946–50,* ed. John A. Garraty and Edward T. James (New York: Charles Scribner's Sons, 1974), 309–11.

58. Edna Johnson, Evelyn R. Sickels, and Frances Clarke Sayers, *Anthology of Children's Literature,* 4th rev. ed. (Boston: Houghton Mifflin, 1959).

59. Judith Saltman, *The Riverside Anthology of Children's Literature,* 6th ed. (Boston: Houghton Mifflin, 1985), 193–96.

60. May Hill Arbuthnot, *The Arbuthnot Anthology of Children's Literature,* rev. ed. (Chicago: Scott Foresman, 1961).

61. Mary M. Burns, "Fall Booklist," *Horn Book* 55 (October 1978): 507–8.

62. Wanda Gág, *Growing Pains: Diaries and Drawings for the Years 1908–1917* (St. Paul: Minnesota Historical Society Press, 1984).

63. Wanda Gág, *The Millions of Cats Day Book,* design Lynn Braswell (New York: Coward, McCann & Geoghegan, 1980).

64. Ruth B. Walter, "Morton Schindel: Creator of Picture Book Parade," *Elementary English* 39 (November 1962): 686.

65. *A Minnesota Childhood: Wanda Gág* (Minneapolis: Heritage Productions, 1984); sound filmstrip.

66. *The Immigrant Experience: Anton Gág* (Minneapolis: Heritage Productions, 1986); videotape.

67. Donald Betts, "Portrait of the Artist as a Young Woman: Eleven Songs from the Diaries of Wanda Gág" (St. Paul: Schubert Club, 1991), SC 103; sound cassette.

68. Public program, *Portrait of the Artist as a Young Woman: Eleven Songs from the Diaries of Wanda Gág* (St. Paul: Minnesota Historical Society and Schubert Club, 1990).

69. Alma Scott (pseud. Georgia Travers), *The Wily Woodchucks,* illus. Flavia Gag (New York: Coward-McCann, 1946).

70. Flavia Gag, *A Wish for Mimi* (New York: Henry Holt, 1958).

71. Eleanor Cameron, "Wanda Gág: Myself and Many Me's," in *The Green and Burning Tree: On the Writing and Enjoyment of Children's Books* (Boston: Atlantic-Little, Brown, 1969), 295–316.

72. Wanda Gág, "The Cry-Away Bird," *Cricket* 3 (August 1976): 6–10.

73. Eleanor Cameron, "I Am Really Alive," *Cricket* 3 (August 1976): 11–15.

74. Martin Quigley, Jr., and Richard Gertner, *Films in America, 1929–1969* (Racine, Wis.: Golden Press, 1970), 92.

75. Stith Thompson, *The Folktale* (New York: Holt, Rinehart and Winston, 1946), 248.

76. C. S. Lewis, *Surprised by Joy: The Shape of My Early Life* (London: Geoffrey Bles, 1955), 57.

77. "Announcements," *Journal of Youth Services to Children* 3 (Winter 1990): 86.

78. Selma G. Lanes, *The Art of Maurice Sendak* (New York: Harry N. Abrams, 1980), 200.

79. Jakob and Wilhelm Grimm, *The Juniper Tree and Other Tales from Grimm,* trans. Randall Jarrell, illus. Maurice Sendak (New York: Farrar, 1973).

80. Audur H. Winnan, *Wanda Gág: A Catalogue Raisonné of the Prints* (Washington, D.C.: Smithsonian Institution Press, 1993).

Selected Bibliography

PRIMARY WORKS

Wanda Gág Special Collections

Readers and viewers can find Wanda Gág's books and fine art in libraries and museums across the country and elsewhere in the world. Specialists seeking her manuscripts, illustrations, and related materials need visit only a few institutions. The executors of the Gág estate and various collectors have selected sites for safekeeping, primarily in Gág's birth state, Minnesota, and Humphreys's birth state, Pennsylvania.

Citizens of Gág's birthplace, New Ulm, Minnesota, are proud of their native daughter; three public institutions hold Gág materials. In the late 1940s, the New Ulm branch of the American Association of University Women purchased a set of Gág's prints and presented them to the New Ulm Public Library. The Brown County Historical Society Museum and Archives collects Gág's childhood and adult drawings as well as correspondence, photographs, and memorabilia; it owns one of the peasant blouses she wore. Collector George Glotzbach intends to bequeath his collection of primary and secondary publications to the museum. In addition, Gág's childhood home is listed in the National Register of Historical Places. A group of local people formed the Wanda Gág House Association in 1988 to renovate the home and furnish it with pieces from the period when the family lived there. The house is open to visitors and serves as the site for educational programs. Flavia Gag's papers are held in the Gary and Norma Harm Private Collection in Minneapolis. Alma (Schmidt) Scott's papers, including the notes for her Gág biography, are located at the Minnesota Historical Society in St. Paul.

The University of Minnesota Children's Literature Research Collections houses first editions of Gág's children's books, most of her children's book manuscripts and illustrations, two scrapbooks, her photograph albums, a draft of her application for a Guggenheim fellowship, some of her correspondence as an adult, and extensive secondary material. *Millions of Cats* manuscripts and illustrations are the most frequently requested by patrons. While the studies for *Nothing at All* are in the CLRC, the glass lithograph plates no longer exist.

Pennsylvania State University at University Park houses the *Tales from Grimm* manuscript and illustrations, and the Detroit Public Library owns the *Snow White and the Seven Dwarfs* final illustrations. The Archives of American Art in New York holds microfilm reels of correspondence from Wanda Gág to Adolf Dehn and the George Biddle papers. Harvard University's Houghton Library has Gág's letters to journalist Lewis Gannett. The Philadelphia Museum of Art keeps Gág's prints, drawings, and printmaking tools. Carl Zigrosser, the curator of prints at the museum after leaving the Weyhe Gallery, arranged for a transfer of Gág's diaries from the museum to the Department of Special Collections at the Van Pelt Library, University of Pennsylvania, where they are now held. The diaries dated from 1917 (the year of her arrival in New York City) to her death in 1946 were first made available for study in 1993. George L. Glotzbach compiled a list of the holdings.

Original or Adapted Fiction

The ABC Bunny. New York: Coward-McCann, 1933.

The Funny Thing. New York: Coward-McCann, 1929.

Gone Is Gone, or The Story of a Man Who Wanted to Do Housework. New York: Coward-McCann, 1935.

Millions of Cats. New York: Coward-McCann, 1928.

Nothing at All. New York: Coward-McCann, 1941.

Snippy and Snappy. New York: Coward-McCann, 1931.

Wanda Gág's Story Book. New York: Coward-McCann, 1932.

Folklore Translations

More Tales from Grimm. New York: Coward-McCann, 1947.

Snow-White and the Seven Dwarfs. New York: Coward-McCann, 1938.

Tales from Grimm. New York: Coward-McCann, 1936.

Three Gay Tales from Grimm. New York: Coward-McCann, 1943.

Wanda Gág's Earth Gnome. Illustrated by Margot Tomes. New York: Coward, McCann & Geoghegan, 1985.

Wanda Gág's Jorinda and Joringel. Illustrated by Margot Tomes. New York: Coward, McCann & Geoghegan, 1978.

Wanda Gág's The Six Swans. Illustrated by Margot Tomes. New York: Coward, McCann & Geoghegan, 1982.

Wanda Gág's The Sorcerer's Apprentice. Illustrated by Margot Tomes. New York: Coward, McCann & Geoghegan, 1979.

Nonfiction

Batiking at Home: A Handbook for Beginners. New York: Crowell, 1926.

Growing Pains: Diaries and Drawings for the Years 1908–1979. New York: Coward-McCann, 1940.

Illustrations

"East of the Sun and West of the Moon." *The Book of Knowledge*. New York: Grolier Society, 1947. 15: 5439–45.

Kellogg, Spencer, Jr. *Autumn Embers*. Eden, N.Y.: Aries Press, 1927.

Rankin, Jean Sherwood. *A Child's Book of Folklore; Mechanics of Written English*. Minneapolis: Augsburg Publishing Company, 1917.

Wigglesworth, Michael. *The Day of Doom, or A Poetical Description of the Great and Last Judgment, with Other Poems*. New York: Spiral Press, 1929.

Essays

"I Like Fairy Tales." *Horn Book* 15 (March–April 1939): 75–80.
"These Modern Women: A Hotbed of Feminists." *Nation* 124 (1927): 691–93.

SECONDARY WORKS

Bader, Barbara. "Wanda Gág." In *American Picture Books from Noah's Ark to the Beast Within*, 32–37. New York: Macmillan, 1976.
Cameron, Eleanor. "Wanda Gág: Myself and Many Me's." In *The Green and Burning Tree*, 295–315. Boston: Little Brown, 1962.
Cox, Richard W. "Wanda Gág: The Bite of the Picture Book." *Minnesota History* 44 (1975): 239–54.
Dobbs, Rose, Ernestine Evans, Alma Scott, Lynd Ward, and Carl Zigrosser. Wanda Gág Memorial Issue. *Horn Book* 23 (1947): 157–207.
Glotzbach, George L. "Wanda Gág Collection Open for Research." *Horn Book* 68 (1992): 122.
Hearn, Michael Patrick. *50 Years of Wanda Gág's Millions of Cats, 1928–1978*. New York: Coward, McCann & Geoghegan, 1978.
_____. *65 Years of Wanda Gág's Millions of Cats, 1928–1993*. New York: Coward, McCann & Geoghegan, 1993.
_____. "Wanda Gág." In *Dictionary of Literary Biography: American Writers for Children, 1900–1960*, edited by John Cech, vol. 22, 179–91. Detroit: Gale, 1983.
Herendeen, Anne. "Wanda Gág: The True Story of a Dynamic Young Artist Who Won't Be Organized." *Century* 116 (1928): 427–32.
Hoyle, Karen Nelson. "A Children's Classic: *Millions of Cats*." *Manuscripts* 31 (Fall 1979): 254–64.
_____. "Introduction to the Reprint Edition." In Wanda Gág, *Growing Pains*, xiii–xxiii. St. Paul: Minnesota Historical Society, 1984.
_____. "Wanda Gág." In *Writers for Children*, edited by Jane M. Bingham, 241–46. New York: Charles Scribner's Sons, 1988.
Kissel, Mary. "Wanda Gág's *Millions of Cats*: Unity through Repetition." *Touchstones* 3 (1989): 54–62.
Klammer, Paul W. *Wanda Gág: An Artist of Distinct Individuality*. New Ulm: Brown County Historical Society, 1979.
Scott, Alma. "Wanda Gág." *Horn Book* (May–June 1947): 159–69.
_____. *Wanda Gág: The Story of an Artist*. Minneapolis: University of Minnesota Press, 1949.
Tebbel, John. *A History of Book Publishing in the United States*. Vol. 3, 171–72, 561–62. New York: Bowker, 1978.
Zigrosser, Carl. "Wanda Gág." In *The Artist in America: Twenty-Four Close-Ups of Contemporary Printmakers*. New York: Knopf, 1942, 33–44.

Index

The Author

Karen Nelson Hoyle is professor and curator of the Children's Literature Research Collections at the University of Minnesota Libraries. Born in Boston, she received her B.A. from St. Olaf College, her M.L.S. from the University of California, Berkeley, and her M.A. and Ph.D. from the University of Minnesota. She teaches a course in the history of children's literature and lectures and writes about immigrant contributors to American children's literature, the international exchange of children's books, and special collections. She is the author of the reference books *Danish Children's Books Published in English* (1983) and *The Kerlan Collection Manuscripts and Illustrations* (1985). A past president of the Children's Literature Association, she has also been a member of the Newbery Award Committee and chairperson of the Caldecott Award and Mildred L. Batchelder Award Committees. She is the recipient of a distinguished achievement award from the Minnesota Library Association, a distinguished alumna award from St. Olaf College, and an honorary doctorate degree from the University of St. Thomas.

The Editor

Ruth K. MacDonald is associate dean of Bay Path College. She received her B.A. and M.A. in English from the University of Connecticut, her Ph.D. in English from Rutgers University, and her M.B.A. from the University of Texas at El Paso. She is author of the volumes on Louisa May Alcott, Beatrix Potter, and Dr. Seuss in Twayne's United States and English Authors Series and of the book *Literature for Children in England and America, 1646–1774* (1982).